Painting with
Brenda Harris

VOLUME 1:
CHERISHED MOMENTS

NORTH LIGHT BOOKS
CINCINNATI, OHIO
www.artistsnetwork.com

Brenda Harris started painting as a hobby at the age of thirty-one. A few years later, encouraged by her family and friends, she entered her first juried art show. Her style and ability to capture one's imagination proved to be a winning combination; she was awarded high honors in the show. She continued to exhibit in shows throughout the country and continued to win numerous awards. However, it was not until she started sharing her techniques with others that her true talent emerged—teaching.

Armed with boundless energy, unlimited patience and a love for painting, she began teaching workshops for a small group of friends in Jacksonville, Florida. From these small but enthusiastic workshops has come an instructor of national television acclaim.

Since 1987 Brenda has taught thousands of students via public television nationwide. In conjunction with each of her many television series, Brenda has authored corresponding instruction books. Brenda has written more than a dozen instructional books and filmed more than 180 educational television shows. She believes that nothing replaces the one-on-one personal touch. Her books and classroom persona, as well as her paintings, reflect her true joy of sharing and attention to detail.

Although Brenda's schedule is demanding, her favorite times still are those spent sharing and teaching in small paint-along workshops.

For more information about Painting With Brenda Harris seminars, books, lesson plans, instructional videos and painting supplies, contact:
Painting With Brenda Harris, P.O. Box 350155, Jacksonville, FL 32235
Phone: (904) 641-1122
Fax: (904) 645-6884
brendaharris@brendaharris.com
www.brendaharris.com

About the Author

Painting With Brenda Harris, Volume 1: Cherished Moments. Copyright © 2005 by Brenda Harris. Printed in Singapore. All rights reserved. No part of this book may be reproduced in any form or by any electronic or mechanical means including information storage and retrieval systems without permission in writing from the publisher, except by a reviewer who may quote brief passages in a review. Published by North Light Books, an imprint of F+W Publications, Inc., 4700 East Galbraith Road, Cincinnati, Ohio 45236. (800) 289-0963. First Edition.

Other fine North Light Books are available from your local bookstore, art supply store or direct from the publisher.

09 08 07 06 05   5 4 3 2 1

Library of Congress Cataloging in Publication Data
Harris, Brenda
Painting with Brenda Harris. Volume 1, cherished moments / Brenda Harris.—1st ed.
    p. cm.
  Includes index.
  ISBN 1-58180-659-0 (pbk. : alk. paper)
  1. Painting--Technique. I. Title: Cherished moments. II. Title.

ND1500.H34 2005
751.4--dc22   2004023642

Edited by Christina Xenos
Interior designed by Barb Matulionis
Production coordinated by Mark Griffin

Metric Conversion Chart

To convert	to	multiply by
Inches	Centimeters	2.54
Centimeters	Inches	0.4
Feet	Centimeters	30.5
Centimeters	Feet	0.03
Yards	Meters	0.9
Meters	Yards	1.1
Sq. Inches	Sq. Centimeters	6.45
Sq. Centimeters	Sq. Inches	0.16
Sq. Feet	Sq. Meters	0.09
Sq. Meters	Sq. Feet	10.8
Sq. Yards	Sq. Meters	0.8
Sq. Meters	Sq. Yards	1.2
Pounds	Kilograms	0.45
Kilograms	Pounds	2.2
Ounces	Grams	28.6
Grams	Ounces	0.035

Destin Dunes
16" × 20" (41cm × 51cm)

Acknowledgments

No matter what your subject, I want to acknowledge with gratitude all devoted teachers for their efforts to make the world a better place through knowledge. Knowledge is the key to opening all doors. By expanding knowledge we can change the world.

To my art teaching pals, Teachers and Educators of Art Materials (TEAM), who have stood by me over the years with encouragement and friendship, I give special thanks. You are like an extended family to me. Although many of us come from different backgrounds and work in many different mediums, we share the same goal: We believe that painting the beauty of nature brings out the best in people. Painting opens your eyes to the beauty around you and makes peo-

ple happy. As art teachers, we strive to make our world a happier place by sharing and teaching as many people as possible the joys and gratification that comes from painting.

Thank you to the terrific staff at North Light Books, especially Christina Xenos, Pam Wissman and Julia Groh, who have been wonderful to work with and made this book possible. Thanks you for your efforts, confidence and support.

To Gary Saltsgiver and the professional staff at WJCT, PBS, Jacksonville, Florida, a big handshake of gratitude. You have been great to work with. Thanks for making the corresponding thirteen-week TV series available for national viewing.

A special thank-you to all of you.

Dedication

I dedicate this book to my loyal students and viewers of my television shows. Without your faithful support over the years, I would not have had the inspiration to continue. Your continued requests for new instructional material encourage me to create.

I also dedicate this book to my beloved family, particularly two very special granddaughters: Breanna and Hollie Ann. I treasure all of you. Thank you for your understanding and loving support over the years.

Last, but not least, I want to acknowledge and dedicate my appreciation to my nephew Clay Collier, attorney-at-law, for working many hours on my behalf—without pay, other than my unfaltering love and appreciation. You are my hero.

Table of Contents

*I*ntroduction

The ability to create your own painting is something that beginning artists yearn to accomplish. By working with the demonstrations in this book, you, too, will feel the creativity stirring inside you. In just one lesson you will be able to paint a beautiful picture that you will be proud to bring home to your loved ones.

You must have a positive attitude: No matter what your goals, your achievement is dependent upon your attitude. A positive attitude is the most important tool of any trade. I put this positive approach into my teaching, and throughout this book I will help you realize that you can become an artist! It's as easy as one, two, three:

1 Study the techniques necessary for the artwork of your choice.

2 Practice until you have developed the skills to execute the techniques to your satisfaction.

3 Achieve the goals you set for yourself.

Nesting Grounds
16" × 20" (41cm × 51cm)

Brenda's Basic Techniques

Throughout this book you will work with patterns (pages 97–109) that you will enlarge for each painting. In some projects you will also use design protectors and mats. This page gives you a reference for these three techniques.

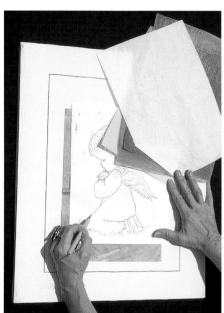

Transferring a Pattern

Enlarge the pattern according to the percentage on it. Lay the canvas on a flat, sturdy surface and tape the pattern firmly in place. Insert a piece of white or black transfer paper powdery side down between the pattern and canvas. Trace the lines with a stylus or a ballpoint pen that no longer writes. While the pattern is still taped in place, lift a corner to check for missed lines.

Remove any visible transfer lines with a kneaded eraser or clean moist sponge after the painting has dried.

Using an Adhesive Design Protector

When you paint the background first, you'll often need to protect an area of your painting. Trace the image you need to protect onto a piece of contact paper or label paper; use the same technique as transferring a pattern. Cut out the image, remove the backing, align the design protector over the traced image and press it onto the dry canvas.

Paint carefully around the protector. Whenever possible, start with the brush on the protector and stroke away from it. Stroking toward the design protector will often force paint under it. When you are ready to paint the image under the protector, carefully peel the protector off the canvas.

French Matting

(1) Place the canvas on a flat surface, then place the mat template (precut photograph matting that can be purchased from any craft or framing store) over it. Hold the mat template securely and trace the inside edges with a waterproof permanent marker or technical pen. (2) Remove the template and let the ink dry. Cover the border with masking or shipping tape, overlapping the tape about ½ inch (12mm) inside the ink lines on all four sides. (3) After the painting is finished, remove the tape to reveal an unpainted border around your painting.

If you would like to create the appearance of double matting, you can use two templates, one with a slightly larger opening. To prevent color seepage under the tape while painting, seal the tape by applying matte medium (clear acrylic paint) over the inside edges of the tape.

Acrylic Paint and Mediums

Acrylic Paint

You can paint with with acrylic tube colors or bottled acrylics. All brands of acrylic paint dry at about the same rate and can be mixed and cleaned up with water. Use cool, clean water when mixing, painting with or cleaning up acrylic paints. Never use oils, thinners or turpentine with acrylics.

Select a brand that is easily accessible and affordable for you. You can set up your palette with colors from several different brands and combine bottled and tube acrylics in the same palette. Most of the colors will not be applied purely from the tube; instead, they will be tinted with white or toned by mixing with other colors.

Acrylics dry at an uneven rate. Often the outer edges of an application begin to dry first; this can cause a spotty appearance. Usually, the color will even out and darken when it is completely dry. Speed the drying with a hair dryer held a few inches away from the canvas. Use a low temperature and keep moving the dryer around above the canvas.

Mediums

You will use acrylic mediums extensively throughout the projects in this book. These mediums let you create beautiful color blends. There are a lot of different acrylic mediums out there besides the three I mention here. Ask your paint supplier for recommendations or contact me to purchase these three directly.

Whiteblend® is excellent for painting wet-into-wet and creating soft, subtle colors. Acrylic paint dries faster and blends better when mixed with it. It can also be used as white acrylic paint, or you can mix it with tube acrylic colors to tint them. Unless otherwise noted, all colors or mixtures should have water or a medium added to them and mixed to the same consistency as Whiteblend.

Clearblend® adds transparency to colors and dries flexible and water-resistant. It appears white but dries clear and is permanent when dry. Use it to create soft edges, transparent glazes and gradual blends and washes. It dries at the same rate as Whiteblend and can also be used in a wet-into-wet wash where you do not want to tint or lighten the colors.

Slowblend® is a clear, slow-drying medium. It dries flexible but less water resistant than Whiteblend or Clearblend. It is also used to slow the drying time primarily in the final layers and details. Add no more than one part Slowblend to two parts paint; too much Slowblend can compromise the paint binder, which causes paint to lift easily from the canvas. Heavy use of Slowblend is not recommended when subsequent layers of paint are to be added.

Acrylic Colors

Mediums

Using a Palette and Mixing Colors

I use the Masterson Super Pro Sta-Wet palette system. It consists of a sponge sheet, special stay-wet palette paper and a durable storage container with a lid. Once you moisten the sponge sheet and lay the palette paper over it, you'll be ready to add colors.

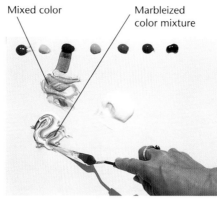

Mixed color   Marbleized color mixture

Adding Paints to Your Palette

Place paints on the palette paper to mix your colors. The paint will stay workable as long as the sponge pad and paper remain wet. As the pad dries out around the edges, the paper will curl. When this happens, lift up a corner of the paper, add water to the dry areas of the sponge pad and press the paper back in place.

To store the mixed paint on your palette, carefully lift the paper off the sponge and lay it to one side. Remove the sponge and squeeze out the water. Replace the sponge, then place the paper with the paint back on the sponge. Place the lid on the tray. Your paints will remain the same for several days. If you plan to save the paint longer and want to avoid a musty odor when you open the box, place the tray in the refrigerator.

Mixing Colors Using Your Palette

I have listed color mixtures in every project in this book. You should mix these before you begin to paint. Mixing colors is an art—not a science! Squeeze out a marble-size dollop of each tube pigment along the edge of your palette paper. Use a clean tapered painting knife to pull out a small amount (about the size of a pea) of your main color. Add other colors in lesser amounts and mix to the shade you want. I prefer to leave the mixture slightly marbleized. This gives a mottled, slightly streaky appearance, which adds interest to paintings. It's up to you to decide exact hues; there are no precise formulas. Often it's best to mix colors directly on the brush or sponge. This is particularly useful when only a small amount is needed or when a gradual change of value or color is desired, such as when you add highlights.

Working With Your Brushes

For brushstrokes and techniques there are many terms that often mean different things to different artists. Some terms are *wet-into-wet*, *wet-on-dry*, *crunching*, *stippling*, *tapping* and *patting*.

Loading a Brush
Have a large container of clean water handy to moisten your brushes before using them. Squeeze the bristles to remove excess water from large brushes; tap smaller brushes on a clean towel. To get a smooth application, load the brush from side to side. Moisten your brushes frequently while painting to insure smooth and even coverage.

Loading a Painting Knife
Hold the edge of the knife in the paint and pull diagonally to load a ribbon of paint on the edge. Use the tapered painting knife to spread the paint in a thin layer across the palette.

Double-Loading
Apply two colors to the brush at one time. Load the brush with the darkest color of the subject, then pull one side of the brush through the highlight color to create a dark and a light side. Position the brush so the stroke is half dark and half light as you move it along the canvas. This technique saves time when used for creating delicate details such as birds or tree limbs.

Side-Loading
Load your brush with medium or water, then blot the excess on a paper towel. Dip one corner of the brush into your paint. Gently stroke the brush back and forth to create a gradation between the paint and water or medium. You should produce a graded color from bold at one end to neutral

Loading a Brush

Loading a Painting Knife

Side-Loading

Crunching

Stippling

at the other. You can also side-load your brush using white and a color or using two colors.

Crunching
Hold the brush perpendicular to the canvas and push straight toward the canvas; then, pushing up, bend the bristles slightly, fanning or flaring the bristles out.

Stippling
Flare the brush before and during loading. Hold the brush perpendicular to the canvas and pounce in the paint, causing the brush to flare open. Tap it against the canvas so it applies random, tiny specks of paints. Then apply less pressure and tap the canvas to distribute speckles of paint.

Tapping and Patting

Angle the brush toward the canvas. Using less pressure than for crunching or stippling, lightly tap a small part of the brush tip on the canvas.

Correcting Mistakes

Don't be afraid of making mistakes; we all do. Anything you put on your canvas can be corrected. Remove wet mistakes using a clean, damp sponge, paper towel or brush. If an error is stubborn to remove, gently agitate it with a toothbrush moistened with Slowblend, then wipe it away. If your mistake has dried, paint over it! Could you cover it with foliage or a cloud? Train yourself to think creatively!

Wet-Into-Wet

Paint a base color, then apply one or more colors directly on the wet base color. Blend the colors together quickly before either dries.

Wet-Next-to-Wet

Apply two acrylic colors next to each other. Blend them together where they meet. This creates a gradual transition between the colors.

Wet-on-Dry

Apply and blend wet acrylic paint over dry acrylic paint. If the color or blend does not suit you, you can remove the wet color with a moist towel or sponge and try again without losing anything.

Wet-on-Sticky, Wet-Next-to-Sticky

Apply and blend wet paint in and around sticky paint (partially dry paint). This technique is frustrating and difficult to control. Slick areas of buildup occur, and other spots lift off the canvas. When this happens, it is best to allow the paint to dry thoroughly, then touch it up by painting wet-on-dry.

Tapping and Patting

Correcting Mistakes

Brushes

You'll need these brushes to complete the projects in this book.

2-inch (51mm) bristle flat
Nos. 4, 8 and 12 bristle flats
¼-inch (6mm) sable/synthetic flat
No. 12 bristle round
No. 2 round
No. 2 liner
1½-inch (38mm) hake or ¾-inch (19mm) mop (Use either of these brushes for blending.)
½-inch (12mm) multitexture (also called a rake or comb)
⅜-inch (10mm) sable/synthetic angle
No. 2 fan
Tapered painting knife
Natural sea sponge

No. 2 round

No. 2 liner

½-inch (12mm) multitexture

No. 2 fan

⅜-inch (10mm) sable/synthetic angle

No. 12 bristle flat

No. 12 bristle round

¾-inch (19mm) mop

2-inch (51mm) bristle flat

Grandpa's Little Angel

Painting people and children, especially profiles, doesn't have to be intimidating, even for a beginner. It helps to think of such paintings as a lot of small parts, much like a puzzle, instead of an intricate painting or a person. When you deal with one section at a time and then connect the sections, you can accomplish any mission you attempt at your easel. You will easily master this composition that way.

Although you will learn the basics of creating hair, skin and clothing folds, you don't have to stay true to the form you see. For example, the eyes are only a suggestion of how eyes should look. The painting is designed to be not a specific portrait but a portrayal of the concept that all children are little angels. After all, aren't all children little angels to their grandparents?

Besides teaching techniques for painting portraits, this painting also teaches you basic feathering techniques when you paint the wings.

Grandpa's Little Angel
20" × 16" (51cm × 41cm)

Materials

Acrylic Colors Burnt Sienna, Burnt Umber, Cadmium Red Medium, Cadmium Yellow Medium, Dioxazine Purple, Payne's Gray, Thalo Green, Titanium White, Ultramarine Blue

Mediums Clearblend, Slowblend, Whiteblend

Brushes 2-inch (51mm) bristle flat, ¼-inch (6mm) sable/synthetic flat No. 2 liner, 1½-inch (38mm) hake or ¾-inch (19mm) mop, ½-inch (12mm) multitexture, ⅜-inch (10mm) sable/synthetic angle, No. 2 fan, Tapered painting knife, Natural sea sponge

Pattern Enlarge the pattern on page 97 133 percent.

Other 20" × 16" (51cm × 41cm) stretched canvas, 20" × 16" (51cm × 41cm) photograph mat (to use as a template), Aerosol acrylic painting varnish, Black transfer paper, Shipping or masking tape, Stylus, Ultrafine-point waterproof permanent marker or technical pen (black or dark brown)

Color Mixtures

Before you begin, prepare these color mixtures on your palette. When you mix the flesh colors and shadows in this project, adjust the amounts of color added to Titanium White to suit your taste.

Medium Violet-Gray	5 parts Whiteblend + 5 parts Payne's Gray + 1 part Dioxazine Purple
Medium Turquoise	12 parts Whiteblend + 2 parts Ultramarine Blue + 1 part Thalo Green
Light Blue	4 parts Whiteblend + 1 part Ultramarine Blue
Teal	Whiteblend + a touch of Thalo Green
Pale Yellow	Whiteblend + a touch of Cadmium Yellow Medium
Pink	Whiteblend + a touch of Cadmium Red Medium
Blush	Titanium White + Cadmium Red Medium
Flesh	Titanium White + a touch each of Cadmium Red Medium, Cadmium Yellow Medium and Burnt Sienna
Flesh Shadow	Flesh mixture + a touch each of Burnt Sienna, Dioxazine Purple and Slowblend
Peach	10 parts Titanium White + 1 part Cadmium Yellow Medium + a touch of Cadmium Red Medium
Off-White	2 parts Titanium White + 1 part Pale Yellow mixture
Light Violet-Gray	1 part Whiteblend + 1 part Medium Violet-Gray mixture
Medium Blue	1 part Whiteblend + 1 part Ultramarine Blue
Tan	1 part Flesh Shadow mixture + a touch of Burnt Umber

1 Paint the Background

Create a French matting border around the canvas (page 7). Transfer the pattern to the canvas (page 7). On the canvas, draw the eyelashes and the ribs in the waistband of the pajamas with an ultrafine-point permanent marker. Let dry. Make a design protector (page 7) and place it over the angel. Apply and blend the six background colors wet-into-wet, using vertical strokes: Start in the top left corner applying the Pink mixture alternately with Whiteblend, ending just behind the head. Add a few strokes of the Pale Yellow mixture in the pink area. Alternate between the Light Blue mixture and Whiteblend to paint the remaining background. Add accents of the Teal, Medium Turquoise and Medium Violet-Gray mixtures. Stroking upward from the bottom. With the Medium Violet-Gray mixture, create a shadowy area around the angel. Blend with vertical strokes using a clean, dry 2-inch (51mm) bristle flat. Let dry.

2 Create the Stars

Using the Off-White mixture and the ½-inch (12mm) multitexture brush, add crosses to indicate stars in the pink area. Turn the brush vertically for the longer, vertical stroke and horizontally for the shorter cross stroke. For the stars in the darker areas of the sky, add a touch of the Medium Blue mixture to the Off-White mixture. Blot the wet stars lightly with your finger to subdue them if needed.

3 Stipple the Ground Using the Background Colors

Begin with the Teal mixture along the top edge, then add the Light Blue mixture and end with the Medium Violet-Gray mixture at the bottom and underneath the angel. Stipple accents of Whiteblend and of the Pink, Pale Yellow and Medium Turquoise mixtures randomly in the wet paint. Let dry. If touch-ups are needed in the background, moisten it with a fifty-fifty mix of water and Clearblend; then add and blend the appropriate colors. Let dry and remove the design protector.

4 Paint the Face, Neck and Ear

Starting at the forehead and moving down to the chin, apply the Flesh mixture along the front of the face with the ⅜-inch (10mm) sable/synthetic angle. Fill in the side of the forehead and face with the Peach mixture. Place a dab of the Blush mixture on the cheekbone and blend. While this is wet, apply and blend a touch of the Flesh Shadow mixture underneath the chin. While the colors are wet, blend them with the feathery tips of the ½-inch (12mm) multitexture brush.

5 Paint the Neck and Ear

Paint the back of the neck with the Flesh Shadow mixture and the inside area with the Flesh mixture. Apply the Flesh Shadow mixture inside the ear and blend toward the face; also apply it behind the ear and blend toward the back of the head. Paint the outer ear with the Pink mixture. Blend with a clean, towel-dried brush. Let dry. Touch up areas on the face by covering them with Clearblend and adding the colors. Blend them into the wet Clearblend as needed. Let dry.

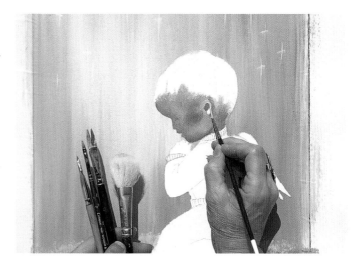

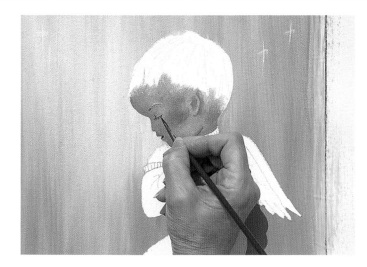

6 Add the Eyebrow and Mouth

Paint light, tiny hair strokes with the no. 2 liner and the Tan mixture to indicate a faint eyebrow. Shadow the mouth with the Tan mixture. Draw a few tiny, thin eyelashes with a no. 2 liner and a watery dark brown mixture of Burnt Umber and Ultramarine Blue.

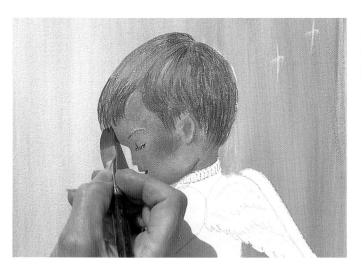

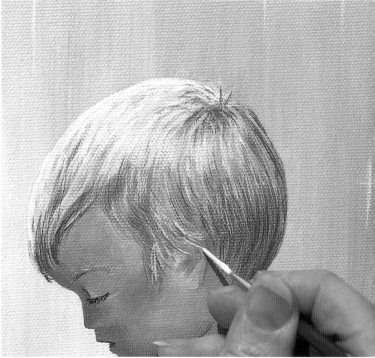

7 Create and Highlight the Hair

Starting at the nape of the neck and moving up, apply the base colors of the hair with the ½-inch (12mm) multitexture brush and overlapping hairlike strokes. Alternate brush-mixing the Flesh and Flesh Shadow mixtures with Burnt Umber for the darker areas. Lighten the hair base color by incrementally adding Cadmium Yellow Medium and Whiteblend for the hair on the top of the head. Let dry. Highlight the hair with hairlike strokes of the Pale Yellow mixture, using the Off-White mixture for the brightest highlights. Add a few detail strands of hair and/or high-lights using the no. 2 liner and the hair colors.

8 Paint the Hand and Feet

Apply the hand and leg paint with the ¼-inch (6mm) sable/synthetic flat. Apply the Flesh Shadow mixture on the right and bottom, the Flesh mixture in the center and the Pink mixture on the left. Use the no. 2 liner with the Flesh Shadow mixture to paint a line between the fingers, and blend slightly with a clean, dry ¼-inch (6mm) sable/synthetic flat. Using a touch of the Peach mixture, highlight on each knuckle and blend. Let dry and touch up if needed.

9 Add the Pajamas

Apply and blend one small section of the pajamas at a time. Alternate painting with the ⅜-inch (10mm) sable/synthetic angle, the ¼-inch (6mm) sable/synthetic flat and the no. 2 liner; then blend with a dry ½-inch (12mm) multitexture brush then a 1½-inch (38mm) hake before moving to the next section. Paint the pajamas with a variety of values of the Medium Blue and Light Blue mixtures, shadowed with the Light Violet-Gray mixture. As you progress, vary the value of the colors by adding more Whiteblend or Ultramarine Blue.

10 Highlight and Blend the Pajamas

Work one section at a time. Cover each section with Clear-blend, then add highlights with the Off-White mixture and the ⅜-inch (10mm) sable/synthetic angle. Blend toward the inside, while wet, with the ½-inch (12mm) multitexture brush. In the same manner, highlight the bands, sleeve, tummy and leg. Dry thoroughly. In the same manner, reapply Clear-blend, then use the Teal mixture for the reflected light along the back, the back of the sleeve and around the leg of the pajamas, blending toward the inside area. Add rib trim details with the no. 2 liner and the pajama colors.

11 *Create the Wings*

Paint, accent and blend one wing at a time, wet-into-wet. Use the ⅜-inch (10mm) sable/synthetic angle to shadow inside the right wing with the Light Violet-Gray mixture, and highlight the outside with Whiteblend. Blend the colors into each other. While this is wet, accent the wing with the Pink and Teal mixtures. Paint the shadow inside the front wing with the ⅜-inch (10mm) sable/synthetic angle. Add Whiteblend around the outer edges. Tap feather marks into the wet paint with Whiteblend and the ½-inch (12mm) multitexture brush. Accent the wet feathers with hints of the Pink, Medium Blue and Teal mixtures. Add dabs of the blue from the pajamas on the edge of the wing where it connects to the fabric, blending to create a gradual connection. Let dry. If you need to touch up the wings, first cover them with Clearblend, then add and blend any or all of the wing colors into the wet Clearblend.

12 *Finishing Touches*

Moisten the ground area with Clearblend. While it is wet, stipple some of the background colors beneath the angel, overlapping the bottom edge of the pajamas using the no. 2 fan. While the area is still wet, add highlights and accents as desired. Sign and let dry. Spray your painting with aerosol acrylic painting varnish. Sit back, smile and be "touched by your angel."

High Perch

Known as the sparrow hawk, the American kestrel lives throughout the United States, migrating as far north as the southern parts of Canada and Alaska and south to the tropics.

The American kestrel is a small hawk that has adapted well to man. They dwell in some of our largest cities and parks, farmlands and open country. It is not uncommon to spot these beautiful birds perched on fences along the highways and byways of the United States.

Because of its unique markings, the American kestrel is a perfect subject to illustrate the uses of technical pens and markers. You will easily use these tools to detail your artwork.

High Perch
20" × 16" (51cm × 41cm)

Materials

Acrylic Colors Burnt Sienna, Burnt Umber, Cadmium Yellow Medium, Dioxazine Purple, Payne's Gray, Raw Sienna, Titanium White, Ultramarine Blue, Yellow Ochre

Mediums Clearblend and Whiteblend

Brushes 2-inch (51mm) bristle flat, No. 2 round, No. 2 liner, 1½-inch (38mm) hake or ¾-inch (19mm) mop, ½-inch (12mm) multitexture, ⅜-inch (10mm) sable/synthetic angle, No. 2 fan, Tapered painting knife, Natural sea sponge

Pattern Enlarge the pattern on page 98 153 percent.

Other 20" × 16" (51cm × 41cm) stretched canvas, Aerosol acrylic painting varnish, Black transfer paper, Paper towels, Stylus, Ultrafine-point waterproof permanent marker or technical pen (black or dark brown)

Color Mixtures

Before you begin, prepare these color mixtures on your palette.

Light Gray	Whiteblend + a touch of Payne's Gray + a touch of Burnt Sienna
Light Blue	20 parts Whiteblend + 1 part Ultramarine Blue + a touch of Payne's Gray
Medium Gray	2 parts Payne's Gray + 2 parts Whiteblend + a speck of Dioxazine Purple
Marbleized Gray-Brown	1 part Burnt Umber + 1 part Payne's Gray + 1 part Whiteblend
Dark Brown	2 parts Burnt Umber + 2 parts Payne's Gray + a touch of Dioxazine Purple
Medium & Light Yellow	1 part Yellow Ochre + 1 part Whiteblend (use more Whiteblend for Light Yellow)
Light Sienna	1 part Whiteblend + 1 part Burnt Sienna
Camel	1 part Raw Sienna + 1 part Whiteblend
Off-White	2 parts Titanium White + a touch of Cadmium Yellow Medium

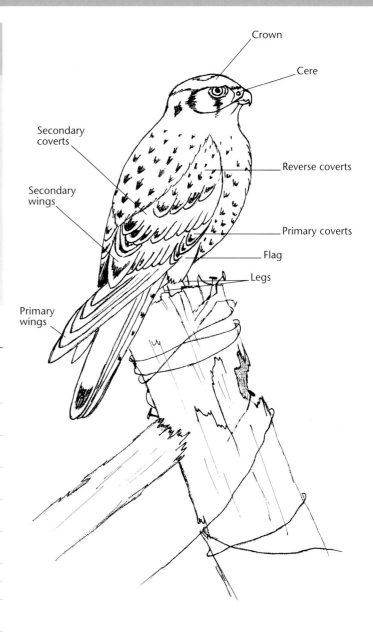

Crown

Cere

Secondary coverts

Reverse coverts

Secondary wings

Primary coverts

Flag

Legs

Primary wings

1 Lay In the Background

Dampen the canvas with water and blot the excess. Apply a generous coating of the Light Gray mixture over the entire canvas with the 2-inch (51mm) bristle flat, adding random dashes of Whiteblend; scrub the paint into the pores of the canvas. Working quickly wet-into-wet, randomly slip-slap (make erratic, overlapping and connecting strokes) some Light Blue mixture in the center. Then add some Medium Gray mixture around the outer edges with the no. 2 fan. Blend with a clean 2-inch (51mm) bristle flat first, then finish with the 1½-inch (38mm) hake or ¾-inch (19mm) mop. Let dry.

2 Transfer the Bird and Post

Transfer the outline of the bird onto the canvas from the pattern (page 7). Apply a thin coating of Whiteblend over the entire bird. Dry thoroughly. Realign the pattern, and then transfer the post.

3 Add the Bird's Markings

Detail the bird's markings using a no. 2 liner loaded with watery Payne's Gray, or you can lay the canvas flat and use a permanent marker or technical pen. Let dry. The markings will show through when you paint.

4 Paint the Eye and Beak

Use the no. 2 liner and no. 2 round to paint and blend the eye, cere and beak. Apply Burnt Umber in the top of the iris and Burnt Sienna in the bottom, blend and dry. Paint the pupil using Payne's Gray. Let dry. Add a touch of Whiteblend for the highlight. Paint and blend the eye ring and cere with the Medium Yellow mixture. Shadow them with Burnt Sienna and highlight them with the Light Yellow mixture. Add the nostril on the cere with thin Burnt Umber.

Paint and blend the beak with the Medium Gray mixture, shadow it with Payne's Gray, and highlight it with the Light Gray mixture and a touch of Whiteblend. Let dry. Add a shadow line under the top beak with thin Payne's Gray and the no. 2 liner. Soften the bottom of the shadow line with the tip of a no. 2 round moistened with Clearblend.

5 Paint and Blend the Head

Paint strokes in the direction of the feathers' growth. A translucent glow of white should show through the paint on the bird's back, primary feathers and tail. Since acrylics darken as they dry, multiple thin applications and drying between applications are preferable to one heavy opaque application.

Use the no. 2 liner and no. 2 round to paint and blend the head. Paint the top of the head with the Medium Gray mixture. Use short feather strokes to highlight and shadow the head, using Whiteblend on the top front section and Payne's Gray on the back. Tap lightly to blend. Let dry. Paint the diamond-shaped marking on the top of the head with thinned Burnt Sienna. Paint the cheek with Whiteblend. Add a speck of Dioxazine Purple to the Medium Gray mixture, then apply a shadow where the bottom of the cheek and eye curve inward; blend these colors together. Highlight the protruding portion of the cheek with short, choppy strokes of Titanium White. Tap lightly to blend. Cast a shadow on the throat using short, choppy, somewhat vertical strokes with the no. 2 liner loaded with the Medium Gray mixture. Fade the color down the chest with Whiteblend. Let dry.

6 Paint the Back

Use the ⅜-inch (10mm) sable/synthetic angle to cover the right side of the back with Clearblend and the left side with Burnt Sienna. Stroke the Burnt Sienna forward over the wet Clearblend; leave the back darker and more opaque and the side lighter and translucent.

7 Paint the Chest

Paint the chest the same way you painted the back. Apply the Camel mixture in the center of the wet chest and Whiteblend on the right. Blend the colors with the no. 2 round using short, tapping strokes. Apply choppy strokes of Titanium White, feathering the marks on the right side of the chest. Add a touch of Payne's Gray and a speck of Dioxazine Purple to the Medium Gray mixture, and apply a shadow on the rump.

8 Paint the Primary and Secondary Coverts

Starting at the top of the wing, paint and blend one section of feathers at a time with the ⅜-inch (10mm) sable/synthetic angle. Using the Medium Gray mixture, apply the shadow along the top and left side of the top three sections, slightly overlapping the bottom edge. Apply the right side and the bottom feather tips using the Light Blue mixture, then blend the colors together. Repeat this for all sections. Let dry. Highlight the feather tips using the no. 2 liner and values of the Light Blue mixture, adding more Whiteblend for the feathers on the right. Let dry.

Use short, choppy strokes and a succession of colors to paint the flag with the no. 2 round. Begin with Burnt Sienna on the left and under the wing, the Camel mixture in the center, and the Light Yellow mixture on the right. Add a few Whiteblend feather marks in the lightest area. Tap lightly to blend slightly. Use the no. 2 liner to paint the left side of the leg with Burnt Sienna and the right side with the Light Yellow mixture. Blend and let dry.

9 Paint the Primary Wings

Paint the right half of the foremost primary feathers with Clearblend. Apply Burnt Umber along the top and left backside of the primary feathers, overlapping into the wet Clearblend. Blend, creating a gradual transition from opaque Burnt Umber to translucent. Let dry. Apply some thin Light Gray mixture highlight on the leading edge of the primary feathers with the no. 2 liner. Add a thin Burnt Umber shadow under the light gray.

10 Paint the Tail

Add Clearblend to the right side of the tail. Apply Burnt Sienna on the left side, overlapping into the wet Clearblend. Blend, creating a gradual transition of the Burnt Sienna from opaque to translucent. Let dry. Paint the right two-thirds of the tail with Clearblend. Mix Burnt Sienna, a touch of Clearblend and a speck of Dioxazine Purple, and apply the mixture along the back of the tail and under the primary feathers with the ⅜-inch (10mm) sable/synthetic angle. Blend toward the inside. Repeat for the shadow down the bird's back. Let dry.

Draw lines separating a few tail feathers with a no. 2 liner and thinned Burnt Umber. Apply Whiteblend along the tip of each tail feather and along the leading edge of the bottom, far right tail feather. Let dry. Shadow the left tips of the white tail feather with the Medium Gray mixture. Use Burnt Umber and the no. 2 liner to paint (or touch up) the markings on the bird's tail, back and chest. Use Payne's Gray on the head and wings, or lay the canvas flat and use the permanent marker.

11 Paint the Fence Posts

Paint one fence post at a time, making all the strokes according to the grain of the wood. Apply Clearblend on the bottoms and in the light areas. Apply the Marbleized Gray-Brown mixture and random dashes of colors from the bird in the dark areas of the posts. Stroke it over the wet areas using Clearblend and the ½-inch (12mm) multi-texture brush, making them progressively translucent as you reach the canvas edges. Streak the sunlit areas with the Camel and Off-White mixtures and Whiteblend, making the highlights blend into the wet shadowed areas. Let dry. Cover the posts with Clearblend. Darken the shadows with the Dark Brown mixture, and highlight the protruding portions in the sunlit areas with dashes of the Off-White mixture and Whiteblend.

12 Detail the Fence Posts

Draw knotholes and cracks in the posts using the no. 2 liner loaded with the Dark Brown mixture. Paint the nails and wire with Burnt Sienna; shadow them with Burnt Umber. Let dry. Moisten the posts with Clearblend. Add streaks of Burnt Sienna using the no. 2 liner for the rust at the base of the nails, then blend the rust downward with a Clearblend-moistened ½-inch (12mm) multitexture brush. Apply shadows at the base of the nails with a translucent mixture of Clearblend and the Dark Brown mixture. Sign the painting, then "perch" yourself in a comfortable spot, sit back, and admire your kestrel. When it is thoroughly dry, spray your painting with an aerosol acrylic painting varnish.

Shrimp Boats Are A-Comin'

Shrimp Boats Are A-Comin'
18" × 24" (46cm × 61cm)

People frequently shy away from painting compositions with many fine details, thinking that only the masters can execute such skilled works. In this project, I will introduce using a ruler and pen to duplicate linework comparable to the precision of the pros. What better subject to illustrate this technique than the rigging of a shrimp boat?

Fortunately, I live near an old fishing village where dozens of shrimp boats line the docks. All of them are worn by years of rough seas and weathered by the wind, rain, blistering hot sun and salty air. I am told that most of the boat owners are also the captains and mechanics. When

something breaks, they figure out a way to engineer a solution. Much of the boats' original equipment has been repaired or replaced with different pieces and parts, making no two shrimp boats alike. The boats have more equipment and rigging than is needed for a good painting. As artists, we have the freedom to simplify and interpret our subjects. This freedom makes painting this old shrimper worry free; you don't need to concern yourself with the exact details of rigging and paraphernalia. Your interpretation of what is there may even be better than mine.

Materials

Acrylic Colors Burnt Umber, Cadmium Yellow Medium, Hooker's Green, Payne's Gray, Thalo Crimson, Titanium White, Ultramarine Blue

Mediums Clearblend, Slowblend, Whiteblend

Brushes 2-inch (51mm) bristle flat, Nos. 4, 8, 12 bristle flats, ¼-inch (6mm) sable/synthetic flat, No. 2 liner, 1½-inch (38mm) hake or ¾-inch (19mm) mop, ⅜-inch (10mm) sable/synthetic angle, No. 2 fan, Tapered painting knife, Natural sea sponge

Pattern Enlarge the pattern on page 99 155 percent.

Other 18" × 24" (46cm × 61cm) stretched canvas, 18" × 24" (46cm × 61cm) photograph mat (to use as a template), Adhesive-backed paper, Aerosol acrylic painting varnish, Black and white transfer paper, Paper towels, Plastic container to hold glaze, Shipping or masking tape, Stylus, Ultrafine-point waterproof permanent marker or technical pen

Color Mixtures

Before you begin, prepare these color mixtures on your palette. Mix the glaze in a separate container.

Sky Blue	4 parts Whiteblend + 2 parts Ultramarine Blue + a touch of Payne's Gray
Hunter Green	3 parts Ultramarine Blue + 3 parts Payne's Gray + 1 part Hooker's Green
Mauve	Whiteblend + 1 part Burnt Umber + a touch each of Payne's Gray and Thalo Crimson
Tan	Whiteblend + a touch each of Cadmium Yellow Medium and Mauve mixture
Off-White	Whiteblend + a touch of Cadmium Yellow Medium
Crimson	6 parts Thalo Crimson + 1 part Burnt Umber + 1 part Whiteblend
Medium Gray-Violet	1 part Whiteblend + 1 part Crimson + 1 part Ultramarine Blue + 1 part Payne's Gray
Forest Green	4 parts Hunter Green +1 part Burnt Umber
Hunter Green glaze	3 parts Clearblend + 1 part Hunter Green mixture

1 French Mat Your Canvas and Transfer the Design

Prepare French matting on your canvas (page 7). Transfer the pattern (except the boat rigging and birds) to the canvas (page 7) so the horizon line is about 9½ inches (24cm) from the top of the canvas. Outline the moldings with an ultra-fine-point waterproof permanent marker or technical pen. Paint inside the windows, doors, hull, the left side of the bow, the tires and the bottom of the boat with Payne's Gray. Let dry. (These will show through the paint and can be touched up easily, as needed.) Create a design protector (page 7) to cover the boat.

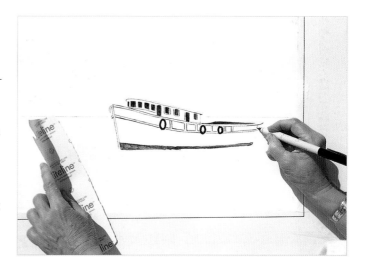

2 Paint the Sky Wet-Into-Wet

Using a 2-inch (51mm) bristle flat, generously cover the sky with Whiteblend, scrubbing briskly and forcing the White-blend into the canvas pores. Without cleaning the brush, add Ultramarine Blue in one of the top corners and a touch of Payne's Gray in the other. Hold the brush horizontally and apply the colors across the top of the wet sky. Apply a few more streaks toward the horizon, making them progressively lighter. Apply streaks of the Mauve mixture in the lower area with a clean no. 12 bristle flat. Blend by stroking horizontally with a clean, dry 2-inch (51mm) bristle flat. Finish blending with the 1½-inch (38mm) hake or ¾-inch (19mm) mop.

3 *Paint the Distant Foliage*

Using a no. 8 bristle flat, brush-mix the Forest Green and Mauve mixtures with Whiteblend creating a mottled light gray-green color. Stipple the distant foliage along the top of the dunes, overlapping the bottom of the wet sky. Apply streaks of that color randomly on the dune below. Create foliage texture by varying the value of the gray-green as you paint. Create misty foliage tops by tapping with a Clearblend-moistened brush or, when dry, by adding more Whiteblend to the foliage color and tapping the top edges.

4 *Form the Sand Dunes*

Paint the sand dunes with the no. 8 bristle flat loaded with the Mauve mixture, connecting it to the foliage in an irregular line. Stroke according to the direction of the slope. Load the no. 2 fan with the Tan mixture and apply highlight streaks on the dune according to the slope. Soften the wet paint between foliage and sand with the no. 2 fan.

5 *Paint the Water*

Apply the base colors for the water using a no. 12 bristle flat. Begin with the Sky Blue mixture in the distant water, then randomly add the Hunter Green mixture, Ultramarine Blue and Payne's Gray incrementally. Brush-mix as you paint to create a gradual transition between light values in the distance to dark values in the foreground water. Add contrasting ripples in the water using the no. 2 fan loaded with the colors you used in the water; you can also add Whiteblend to the colors. Blend with the no. 2 fan, using choppy, curved interconnecting strokes.

6 *Paint the Mast and Booms*

Realign the pattern and transfer the booms, mast, rigging, pulleys and details, using both white and black transfer paper. Apply the mast and booms with the no. 2 liner and a mixture of Payne's Gray, water and a touch of Slowblend. Use the no. 2 liner and various values of the Mauve, Medium Gray-Violet or Crimson mixtures for the base colors of the other equipment. (Don't paint the rigging yet.)

7 _Add the Wheelhouse_

Apply a shadow with the ¼-inch (6mm) sable/synthetic flat and a dark mixture of Payne's Gray and the Mauve mixture underneath the wheelhouse roof. Add Whiteblend incrementally to the Payne's Gray and the Mauve mixture to paint the wheelhouse, leaving it darker along the front curved portion and lighter on the side. Let dry. Touch up the windows and doors with Payne's Gray. Paint the roof, window and door moldings with the Off-White mixture and the no. 2 liner, and shadow them with a darker value of the wheelhouse color. Let dry.

8 _Embellish the Equipment_

Add Payne's Gray to the items' base color for shadows on the bottom and/or left side of each object. Highlight the top and/or right side with the Off-White mixture, and blend the colors together.

9 _Paint the Hull_

Use the Crimson mixture loaded on the ⅜-inch (10mm) sable/synthetic angle to paint the band around the top of the hull. Highlight the central area by adding a touch of Cadmium Yellow Medium and Whiteblend to the Crimson mixture. Add the moldings along the top, bottom and sides of the crimson band using the no. 2 liner loaded with the Off-White mixture, then shadow them with thinned Payne's Gray.

10 Shadow the Hull

Use the ⅜-inch (10mm) sable/synthetic angle and a mix of Whiteblend and Payne's Gray with the Mauve and Crimson mixtures to paint the shadows on the hull below the crimson band. This color should be slightly darker than the shadow on the front of the wheelhouse. Apply the Off-White mixture over the remaining side of the hull so it overlaps into the wet shadows; blend these colors together.

11 Detail the Hull

Paint the bowsprit with the no. 2 liner, placing the Mauve mixture on the right side and a Payne's Gray shadow on the left. Paint the tires using Payne's Gray loaded on the no. 2 liner. Draw a bracket or rope attaching the tires to the top hull molding. Add Whiteblend to the brush and highlight them with a medium-gray value. Create a translucent mixture of Clearblend and Payne's Gray, then apply a shadow to the left of each tire and any remaining moldings on the wheelhouse and boat. Blot if they become too opaque. Let dry. Paint the band around the bottom of the boat with Payne's Gray highlighted in the center with the Crimson mixture.

12 Apply the Rigging

Use either the no. 2 liner, ultrafine-point permanent marker or technical pen. When using a pen, lay the canvas faceup on a flat surface and use ultrafine tips for the thin rigging lines. Use a ruler for straight lines and freehand the curved ones. When using the no. 2 liner, keep the canvas elevated and use a thin mixture of Payne's Gray and Slowblend. Correct crooked lines while they are wet with a dry ⅜-inch (10mm) sable/synthetic angle. Let dry.

13 *Detail the Water*

Moisten the water with Clearblend and apply Hunter Green glaze over the foreground water up to the bottom of the boat and blend it beyond the boat with the no. 2 fan. Load the no. 2 fan with the Off-White mixture and crunch splashes of water randomly along the bottom of the boat. Pull the bottom of the off-white splashes down into the wet glaze. Make curved strokes, connecting the splash to the water movement and the wet glaze around the bottom of the boat. Add the foreground water movement using a no. 2 fan loaded with a mixture of Ultramarine Blue and Whiteblend. Move the brush according to the water direction. Let dry. Touch up the distant water by covering it with Clearblend and adding the appropriate colors while wet. Let dry.

14 *Add the Birds*

Paint the birds with a double-loaded no. 2 liner. Use the Medium Gray-Violet mixture and Whiteblend for the distant birds, and use the Hunter Green mixture and Whiteblend for the birds in the foreground. Use thin Payne's Gray to apply beaks and wing tips on the foreground birds. Sign your painting with the no. 2 liner. Let dry. Remove the masking tape. If wet paint has seeped under the tape, remove it with a clean moist sponge. If the paint is dry, moisten it and scrape the excess off with a painting knife or sharp-edged instrument, and then paint over it with Whiteblend. Dry thoroughly. Spray the painting with aerosol acrylic painting varnish and sing along with me, "Shrimp boats are a-comin'—la-la-la-la-la-la..."

Destin Dunes

Destin Dunes
16" × 20" (41cm × 51cm)

When I paint sand dunes, I think of how vital they are to the survival of our shorelines. They work as shock absorbers, protecting homes and habitats from the impact of ocean waves, salt, spray and sand.

This particular sand dune painting is based on memories of vacations spent in Destin, Florida; however, the scene could be at almost any southern beach. I chose this particular composition because it gives you a chance to paint many elements of the shoreline: water, waves and incoming tide, with both flat and huge sand dunes, sea oats (the tall grasses that grow in the sand dunes) and gulls.

These techniques are not limited to painting seascapes; they can be equally useful in painting inland scenes. For instance, the technique for creating clouds is universal. The sand dune and grass techniques could easily be used to create drifting snowbanks around wheat stubble. Use your imagination and have fun!

Materials

Acrylic Colors Burnt Umber, Cadmium Yellow Medium, Cerulean Blue, Hooker's Green, Payne's Gray, Thalo Crimson, Titanium White

Mediums Clearblend and Whiteblend

Brushes 2-inch (51mm) bristle flat, Nos. 4, 8 and 12 bristle flats, No. 12 bristle round, No. 2 liner, 1½-inch (38mm) hake or ¾-inch (19mm) mop, ½-inch (12mm) multitexture, ⅜-inch (10mm) sable/synthetic angle, No. 2 fan, Tapered painting knife, Natural sea sponge

Pattern Enlarge the pattern on page 100 154 percent.

Other 16" × 20" (41cm × 51cm) stretched canvas, Aerosol acrylic painting varnish, Black and white transfer paper, Paper towels, Stylus

Color Mixtures

Before you begin, prepare these color mixtures on your palette.

Light Blue	10 parts Whiteblend + 1 part Cerulean Blue
Hunter Green	5 parts Cerulean Blue + 5 parts Payne's Gray + 1 part Hooker's Green
Light Gray	10 parts Whiteblend + 1 part Payne's Gray
Gray-Green	3 parts Hunter Green mixture + 1 part Light Gray mixture
Mauve	10 parts Whiteblend + 5 parts Payne's Gray + 1 part Thalo Crimson + 1 part Cerulean Blue + 1 part Burnt Umber
Medium Gray	2 parts Payne's Gray + 2 parts Mauve mixture + a touch of Whiteblend
Pale Peach	Whiteblend + a touch of Cadmium Yellow Medium + a touch of Thalo Crimson
Pale Yellow	Whiteblend + a touch of Cadmium Yellow Medium

1 Create the Sky

Use the pattern to transfer the water and dune design to the canvas (page 7). Make the horizon line 3 inches (8cm) above the bottom of the canvas. Use a generous amount of paint and scrub briskly when applying the sky colors using the 2-inch (51mm) bristle flat. Paint the Light Blue mixture in the top third of the sky. Add Whiteblend incrementally to the same brush to lighten the value, making the sky gradually lighter as it reaches the water line. Stroke horizontally to blend. Create large billowing cloud shapes in the top three-quarters of the wet sky by loading the Light Gray mixture on the corner of the 2-inch (51mm) bristle flat. Occasionally, alter the clouds' values and colors by adding a touch of the Mauve or the Light Blue mixture to the paint on the brush.

2 Blend the Clouds

Blend the billows and overall sky with a dry 1½-inch (38mm) hake or ¾-inch (19mm) mop. Use the no. 2 fan or the side edge of a no. 12 bristle flat to apply horizontal streaks along the bottom of the large billows and the sky. Add more background sky paint to facilitate blending as needed. Let dry.

3 Highlight the Clouds

Apply then blend each cloud highlight one at a time. Generously load Clearblend on the no. 12 bristle round. Gently wipe the brush across a paper towel to remove excess globs. Barely dip the tip of the brush in both Whiteblend and a touch of the Pale Peach mixture. Tap the brush lightly on the palette to distribute the paint evenly. Hold the brush at an angle—almost flat—against the canvas with the handle pointing down. Tap to create the top edges of the billows, creating a variety of sizes, shapes and values. Tap the brush inside the cloud, skipping spaces to create the illusion of depth. Scumble or scrub the heel of the brush to blend the inside and bottoms of the clouds; frequently clean and reload your brush. Blend all clouds slightly with the 1½-inch (38mm) hake or ¾-inch (19mm) mop. Apply less highlight paint on the clouds along the sides of the canvas as well as toward the horizon. Blend away unwanted hard edges or excess highlights using a clean brush loaded with Clearblend.

4 Paint the Ocean and Beach

Paint the ocean using the sky and cloud colors, adding the Gray-Green mixture to darken the central water area. Blend these colors together. Apply ruffled streaks of the Hunter Green mixture to suggest the waves, blending the bottoms into the ocean's colors. Paint the flat area of the beach, alternating between the Mauve mixture and Whiteblend. Blend, connecting the ocean and sand. Let dry.

5 Add the Whitecaps and Receding Tide

Moisten the ocean with Clearblend. Apply and blend whitecaps or foam patterns by creating irregular lines of Whiteblend along the wave tops using the no. 2 liner. Blend the side edges of the whitecap horizontally across the wave. Create the curl under the crashing whitecaps by stroking the bottom edge in an elongated C. The bottom of the C runs parallel across the canvas. Make the distant waves flatter and smaller by using less paint and smaller, flatter strokes. Let dry.

Moisten the beach and foreground water with Clearblend. Using the no. 2 liner, apply a streak of Whiteblend horizontally across the moistened beach, where the water and sand merge. Starting on the top edge of the tide line, stroke horizontally to blend it with a clean ½-inch (12mm) multitexture brush. Make each subsequent blending stroke higher on the canvas, blending the Whiteblend tide line gradually into the ocean. Repeat for additional tide lines.

6 Paint the Dune Base

Block in the light areas by applying Whiteblend and the Pale Peach mixture alternately with a clean ⅜-inch (10mm) sable/synthetic angle. Paint the shadowy portions of the dunes and foreground sand with the 2-inch (51mm) bristle flat, alternating between the Mauve, Light Gray and Medium Gray mixtures. Blend slightly by stroking in the direction of the drifts in the sand with a clean 2-inch (51mm) bristle flat, leaving a mottled appearance and lots of light and dark streaks. Slightly soften the brush marks with the 1½-inch (38mm) hake or ¾-inch (19mm) mop. Let dry.

7 Highlight the Dunes

Apply Clearblend over the center dune, then add and blend reflected lights while the Clearblend is wet. Marbleize Titanium White and the Pale Peach mixture using the ⅜-inch (10mm) sable/synthetic angle, then dab and streak it along the top left side and in some areas inside the large center dune. As needed, touch up or add shadows and colors. Blend slightly, leaving the illusion of lumpy sand on the crest and changing to smooth drifts and flat sand.

8 Dune Reflected Lights

Reapply Clearblend if the dune starts to dry. Apply streaks of the Light Blue mixture with a clean ⅜-inch (10mm) sable/synthetic angle to create the reflected light in the shadow areas. Follow the contour of the sand and blend the colors using the no. 2 fan. If needed, strengthen the shadows around the highlights using the Medium Gray or Mauve mixture, then blend slightly. Use much less paint but the same technique to apply reflected light, and if needed, highlight on the right side of the distant dune.

9 Create the Grass Clusters

Create clusters of thin wispy grass along the top and middle of the center dune using a ½-inch (12mm) multitexture brush loaded with a soupy thin mixture of the Hunter Green mixture and a touch of Burnt Umber. Applying very little pressure on the tip of the brush, add some Light Gray mixture to the grass to create a medium gray-green. Paint shorter, lighter-value grasses on the distant dune. Brush-mix the Pale Yellow mixture with water to a soupy consistency. Load that onto a ½-inch (12mm) multitexture brush and highlight the grass. Let dry. Transfer the fence and birds to the canvas from the pattern.

10 Add the Sand, Fence and Tall Grass

Add the fence and grass details using the no. 2 liner. Paint the fence of the center dune with the Dark Gray mixture and highlight it with Whiteblend. Make the fence slats progressively lighter, shorter and closer together going to the right and on the distant dune. Save time by double-loading the no. 2 liner. Apply the fence wire with watery shades of the Medium Gray mixture. Make the taller grass blades using all the grass colors and painting in an upward stroke. Apply shorter, lighter-value grass in the distance. Overlap some fence slats with shorter grass.

11 Paint the Birds

Double-load the Medium Gray mixture and Whiteblend onto a no. 2 liner to paint the birds. Let dry. Add the birds' eyes and primary feathers with thinned Payne's Gray. Paint orange beaks on the two larger birds using a brush mixture of Cadmium Yellow Medium, a touch of Thalo Crimson and the Pale Peach mixture.

12 Speckle the Foreground Dune

Speckle the foreground dune with any or all of the colors from your painting. Load each color plus water onto a no. 2 fan. Turn the bristles toward the canvas and scrape over them to flick tiny splatters of color using your finger or a tapered painting knife.

13 *Final Details*

Apply the suggestion of shells on the shadowed side of the foreground dune using dabs of the Light Gray mixture loaded on a no. 2 liner. Add Whiteblend to the same brush and apply lighter shells on the sunlit side. Let dry. Apply shadows behind the dabs using the no. 2 liner loaded with a thin, translucent mixture of Clearblend and Payne's Gray. Use the same shadow mixture to apply shadows from the fence slats across the dune. Make the fence shadows follow the contour of the sand. Blot them occasionally to subdue the shadows. Sign your name and let the painting dry. Spray your painting with aerosol acrylic painting varnish. Take a break and allow your imagination to take you for a stroll on your warm sunny beach!

Someplace I've Been

Someplace I've Been
14" × 18" (36cm × 46cm)

This painting, which represents no particular place, is a perfect setting to demonstrate the focus of this lesson: using a basecoat as a foundation to simplify the execution of a painting. I find painting on a basecoated canvas fun and enjoyable. This technique eliminates a great deal of your work by using the basecoat to provide some of the painting's color.

Repetition will serve you well. Your performance as an artist will grow quickly with practice and experimentation, so think of this painting as a rehearsal. Try using this technique in different compositions of your own. Or try this same composition or one of your own using a different basecoat color; use any color you choose! Simply select a color of dominance for your painting, then basecoat your surface with that color. As you paint, allow the color to show through in appropriate areas throughout. With a little practice, you will find it a quick, fun and easy way to paint creatively.

Materials

Acrylic Colors   Burnt Umber, Cadmium Red Medium, Cadmium Yellow Medium, Dioxazine Purple, Hooker's Green, Payne's Gray, Thalo Yellow Green, Titanium White, Ultramarine Blue

Mediums   Clearblend and Whiteblend

Brushes   2-inch (51mm) bristle flat, ¼-inch (6mm) sable/synthetic flat, No. 12 bristle round, No. 2 liner, 1½-inch (38mm) hake or ¾-inch (19mm) mop, ⅜-inch (10mm) sable/synthetic angle, No. 2 fan, Tapered painting knife, Natural sea sponge

Pattern   Enlarge the pattern on page 101 153 percent.

Other   14" × 18" (36cm × 46cm) stretched canvas, Adhesive-backed paper, Aerosol acrylic painting varnish, Black transfer paper, Stylus

Color Mixtures

Before you begin, prepare these color mixtures on your palette.

Blue-Black	1 part Burnt Umber + 1 part Ultramarine Blue + 1 part Payne's Gray + a touch of Dioxazine Purple
Blue-Green	2 parts Ultramarine Blue + 1 part Thalo Yellow Green + 1 part Whiteblend
Medium Green	1 part Hunter Green mixture + 2 parts Whiteblend
Celery	6 parts Whiteblend + 1 part Thalo Yellow Green + 1 part Hunter Green mixture
Gray-Green	4 parts Violet-Gray mixture +1 part Hunter Green mixture
Hunter Green	3 parts Payne's Gray + 3 parts Ultramarine Blue + 1 part Hooker's Green
Light Green	2 parts Whiteblend + 1part Celery mixture + 1 part Thalo Yellow Green
Medium Dusty Violet	2 parts Violet-Gray mixture + 1 part Blue-Black mixture + a touch of Dioxazine Purple
Medium Gray	Violet-Gray mixture + Blue-Black mixture
Peach	4 parts Whiteblend + 1 part Titanium White + a touch of Cadmium Yellow Medium + a touch of Cadmium Red Medium
Violet-Gray	20 parts Whiteblend + 5 parts Payne's Gray + 1 part Dioxazine Purple
Light Blue	Whiteblend + Ultramarine Blue (create various values)

1   Paint the Background and Bridge Shadow

Using the 2-inch (51mm) bristle flat, paint the canvas with the Violet-Gray mixture. Let dry. Transfer the design to the canvas, placing the top of the bridge 5¼-inches (13cm) from the bottom (page 7). Place a design protector over the bridge (page 7). Using the Blue-Black mixture, paint horizontal strokes with the ⅜-inch (10mm) sable/synthetic angle for the reflection of the bridge's shadow. Let dry.

2   Create the Distant Trees

Scrub a generous coating of Clearblend onto the sky and background foliage area with the 2-inch (51mm) bristle flat. Apply the Peach mixture to the top of the sky and to the bottom of it behind the treetops. Apply the Violet-Gray mixture between the peach streaks and blend with a ¾-inch (19mm) mop or 1½-inch (38mm) hake. Tap a clean moist sponge along the bottom of the peach color to lift and disperse it, creating the illusion of distant, muted treetops. Tap out irregular heights and shapes of treetops. If hard edges occur and the treetops are difficult to lift out, apply them with the Violet-Gray mixture loaded on the sponge.

3 Paint Darker Foliage and the Distant Riverbank

Create a progression of darker, lower foliage on the far side of the bridge by adding small amounts of the Violet-Gray, Gray-Green and Hunter Green mixtures, to the sponge. Begin with the Violet-Gray mixture for the sparse, taller foliage. Add the Gray-Green mixture, then apply shorter, darker foliage along the top of the bridge and under the arch of the bridge and a few random taller trees, using more paint and tapping harder at the foliage base to create density. Add increments of the Hunter Green mixture to darken the foremost foliage behind the top right side of the bridge. Paint the distant riverbank (located in the arch of the bridge) with the no. 2 fan and Clearblend. Brush-mix and apply the Medium Gray mixture across the riverbank, following the lay of the land. Add the Peach mixture to the Medium Gray mixture in the no. 2 fan and apply streaks of a dull peach highlight across the riverbank. Blend slightly.

4 Create the Foliage Reflections

Apply Clearblend over the water area with the no. 12 bristle round. Stroking horizontally into the wet Clearblend with the ⅜-inch (10mm) sable/synthetic angle, alternately apply the Hunter Green and Blue-Black mixtures adjacent to the riverbank and in the dark areas of the water. Stroking vertically with the no. 2 fan, apply the Light Blue mixture in the lighter areas of the water, overlapping and blending into the dark colors slightly. Add a dash of the Peach mixture next to the bridge's shadow on the extreme right, creating the brightest area in the water. Blend slightly. Using a clean no. 2 fan and cleaning the brush between strokes, create the appearance of shimmer with short zigzag, horizontal strokes, placing each subsequent stroke lower.

5 Paint and Blend the Bridge Wet-Into-Wet

Paint the bridge with Clearblend. Using the ⅜-inch (10mm) sable/synthetic angle. Dab colors into the wet Clearblend allowing some of the basecoat to show through, creating a mottled, stone appearance. Dab the Peach mixture to the top right two-thirds of the bridge. Create a progression of darker values on the bridge by incrementally dabbing the Violet-Gray and Medium Dusty Violet mixtures in and around the peach and remaining areas. Add dabs of the Hunter Green mixture in the foliage shadow areas. Dab with a clean ⅜-inch (10mm) sable/synthetic angle to blend slightly, applying more Clearblend as needed. Let dry.

6 Create a Shadow and Define the Stones

Moisten the shadowed arch underneath the bridge with Clearblend. Highlight the leading edge of the arched opening on the far side of the bridge with the no. 2 liner, alternating between the Violet-Gray and Peach mixtures. Tap faint images of stones on the bridge shadow with the Medium Gray mixture. Blot to subdue the stones in the shadow. Let dry.

7 Detail the Bridge

Using the ⅜-inch (10 mm) sable/synthetic angle, cover the bridge with Clearblend. About ¼ inch (6mm) from the top, use the Medium Dusty Violet mixture (darken the value if needed) to apply a shadow across the bridge, leaving a band along the top. Blend the bottom of the shadow using a Clearblend-moistened no. 2 fan. Separate the band into individual stones, irregularly shaped and sized, using the no. 2 liner loaded with the shadow color.

8 Create the Foreground Foliage

Use the Hunter Green mixture loaded on a sponge to tap foreground foliage in front of both sides of the bridge, making the left side taller. Let dry. Protect the bridge with a piece of paper when tapping reflected highlights and flowers in darker foliage behind the bridge. Use the Blue-Green mixture to tap reflected light in the dark foliage areas. Use a sponge loaded with the Medium Green mixture to tap foliage highlights to the tops of the dark foliage clusters on right side of the canvas. Add the Celery mixture to the sponge and tap a lesser amount of highlight along the top of the medium-green foliage highlights, making the foliage "grow" slightly. Likewise, apply a smaller amount of the Light Green mixture to the top of the Celery mixture. Let dry.

9 *Paint the Flowers and Their Reflections*

Lightly tap Cadmium Red Medium flowers on the right side of the bridge base using a clean sponge. Add Titanium White to the sponge and lightly tap a few highlights. Add Dioxazine Purple to the paint on the sponge to create the base color of the violet flowers on both sides of the foliage. Add a touch of Titanium White to the Dioxazine Purple to create the highlight, making the highlights more pronounced on the right side of the bridge. Protect the bridge with a piece of paper. Add some Violet-Gray mixture to all flower colors, and apply distant flowers in the foliage behind the bridge. Moisten the water with Clearblend, then lightly tap the flowers' respective reflected colors directly beneath it. Stroke downward then horizontally over the reflected color with a no. 2 fan moistened with Clearblend. Let dry.

10 *Apply the Leaves and Petals*

Using the ¼-inch (6mm) sable/synthetic flat, apply a few defined leaves and petals on the foremost foliage and flowers, concentrating these predominately on the right side of the bridge. Brush-mix and apply three values of leaves on the foliage incrementally using Thalo Yellow Green and Titanium White. Add dabs or blooms on the foreground flowers with a brush mixture of the flowers' respective colors and highlights.

11 *Add the Tree Trunks and Birds*

Paint tiny twigs and tree trunks in the foliage with a no. 2 liner double-loaded with the Medium Dusty Violet and Peach mixtures. Paint the distant birds with a no. 2 liner double-loaded with Whiteblend and the Medium Dusty Violet mixture.

12 *Paint the Final Details*

Cover the water with Clearblend, using a no. 2 fan. Use the no. 2 liner or a tapered painting knife to apply thin, horizontal water lines at the base of the bridge and flowers. Load a no. 2 fan with Clearblend to soften the lines with light horizontal strokes. Let dry. Sign your name and admire your painting. Spray your masterpiece with aerosol acrylic painting varnish. Pat yourself on the back and think of all the wonderful things you would like to paint! Think positively and you can "cross that bridge when you come to it."

Snow's on the Way

Snow's on the Way
18" × 24" (46cm × 61cm)

The day I created this painting, I was in my Florida studio and could hear the honking of geese flying in for the winter. Their honking reminded me of a cold, rainy fall day in Connecticut. I recalled the chill of the wind and the sight of the migratory birds taking flight to escape the bitter cold winter that was approaching. I knew for sure that "snow's on the way!"

With this feeling and image in mind, I started to paint. I wanted to convey the urgency caused by the wind and cold yet make the painting warm and inviting. I realized a good way to express my thoughts and mood would be to make a bold statement with soft pastel colors. I then chose a soft pastel mauve for the general tone of my painting.

In previous projects, I have taught you the ease of painting on a basecoated canvas and how to give your painting a designer's flair by adding a French matted border. Now, I want to take you a step further. We are going to color-coordinate the painting with our the border, where we previously stopped short and used the white of the canvas for the border. This painting is designed to communicate my frame of mind and to teach all these combined techniques.

To give us a head start, we use the same color for the border and the basecoating of the painting. It is less work and insures that the painting and border harmonize.

Materials

Acrylic Colors Burnt Umber, Cadmium Yellow Medium, Dioxazine Purple, Payne's Gray, Thio Violet, Titanium White

Mediums Clearblend and Whiteblend

Brushes 2-inch (51mm) bristle flat, No. 12 bristle flat, No. 12 bristle round, No. 2 round, No. 2 liner, 1½-inch (38mm) hake or ¾-inch (19mm) mop, ½-inch (12mm) multitexture, ⅜-inch (10mm) sable/synthetic angle, No. 2 fan, Tapered painting knife, Natural sea sponge

Pattern Enlarge the pattern on page 102 153 percent.

Other 18" × 24" (46cm × 61cm) stretched canvas, 18" × 24" (46cm × 61cm) photograph mat (to use as a template), Aerosol acrylic painting varnish, Cutting tool, Masking and shipping tape, Transfer paper, Waterproof permanent marker or technical pen

Color Mixtures

Before you begin, prepare these color mixtures on your palette.

Barely Pink	Whiteblend + a speck of Thio Violet
Cream	Whiteblend + a touch of Cadmium Yellow Medium + a speck Thio Violet
Dark Brown	1 part Burnt Umber + 1 part Payne's Gray + 1 part Pale Violet-Gray mixture
Light Mauve	50–60 parts Whiteblend + 1 part Thio Violet + 1 part Burnt Umber + 1 part Payne's Gray
Pale Violet-Gray	60 parts Whiteblend + 10 parts Payne's Gray + 1 part Dioxazine Purple
Warm Brown	1 part Burnt Umber + 1 part Thio Violet + 1 part Cadmium Yellow Medium

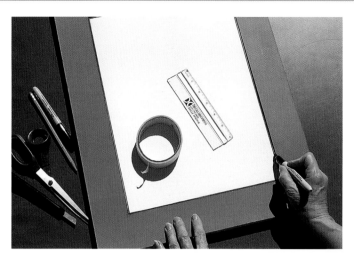

1 Outline the Mat

Place the canvas face up on a flat surface. Align the mat with the canvas edges and use a permanent marker or technical pen to trace the opening. Hold the mat securely in place as you slowly pull the technical pen along the edges. Repeat if you prefer a bolder mark. Let dry.

2 Tape the Edges

Remove the mat and cover all four lines with 1-inch (25mm) masking tape, positioning pieces of tape to extend ⅜ inch (10mm) inside the lines. The pieces of tape should overlap, crossing at the corners. Use a ruler to intersect the middle of the angle where the tape crosses; draw a line across the top piece of tape. Repeat for each corner.

3 Remove Excess Tape

Cut along the line you drew in step 2 to miter the top piece of tape at the corner. (When using scissors, lift the tape at that corner and cut. When using a blade or knife, align the cutting edge along the mark [at the 45° angle], then pull the tape against the blade.) Lift and separate the tape at that corner. Place the mitered piece down first with the uncut piece on top. Cut the top piece of tape so that it does not extend outside the matted area, but slightly overlaps the mitered piece to prevent seepage. This creates a perfect rectangle of tape with no extending ragged edges. With one hand on the back and the other directly opposite it on the front, press to secure the tape.

4 Lay a Base Color on the Canvas

Using a 2-inch (51mm) bristle flat, paint the canvas and tape with Clearblend to seal the edges and prevent paint seepage during the basecoating and painting processes. Let dry. With a clean 2-inch (51mm) bristle flat, paint the canvas and tape with the Light Mauve mixture. Let dry. If the first application dries unevenly or produces streaking, apply a second application. Let dry.

5 Cover the Border With Tape

Cover the outside border with wider shipping or masking tape, adding strips of tape if needed to cover the entire border. Turn the canvas horizontally and transfer the water line from the pattern so that it is 1½-inches (38mm) above the inside of the 1-inch (25mm) tape edge.

6 Paint the Sky Wet-Into-Wet

Slightly moisten the sky area with the 2-inch (51mm) bristle flat and water. Blot away excess water. Using the same brush, apply a generous application of Clearblend over the moist sky area. Using the no. 2 fan, apply random splotches of the Pale Violet-Gray mixture into the wet Clearblend. Apply splotches of the Light Mauve, Barely Pink and Cream mixtures in the lower parts of the wet sky, making the color less dense as you move up.

7 Blend the Sky

Blend the splotches into the wet Clearblend with erratic strokes, creating a blustery effect. First use a clean, dry 2-inch (51mm) bristle flat, then smooth and soften the strokes with the 1½-inch (38mm) hake.

8 Add the Foliage

Shield the water with a piece of paper, then, using a no. 12 bristle round or flat, stipple the foliage above the water line with the Pale Violet-Gray mixture, creating lacy edges and texture.

9 Paint the Water

Apply Clearblend on the water area. Paint streaks of the Light Mauve, Barely Pink and Cream mixtures horizontally across the top of the water and the Pale Violet-Gray mixture across the bottom of the water, using the no. 2 fan. Blend slightly with a clean, dry no. 2 fan. Let dry. Transfer the trees, grass and geese to the canvas from the pattern.

10 Create Twigs and Sticks

Load the no. 2 liner with very thin Pale Violet-Gray mixture and create short wispy twigs and sticks coming out of the foliage. Blot the base of the twigs to blend them into the foliage. Double-load the no. 2 liner with the Pale Violet-Gray mixture (for the shadow color) and the Light Mauve mixture (for the highlight). Hold the no. 2 liner with the Pale Violet-Gray mixture on the right and paint the trees and limbs. Alternate using the Barely Pink mixture for the Light Mauve mixture. Reload the brush frequently.

11 Paint the Geese

Use the no. 2 liner, ⅜-inch (10mm) sable/synthetic angle and no. 2 round to paint the geese. Use the Pale Violet-Gray mixture to lay a basecoat on the geese, adding a touch of Whiteblend to distinguish the edge of their foremost wings. Paint their feet, beaks and eyes using a no. 2 liner loaded with thinned Payne's Gray. Create reflected light on the top edge of the beaks and feet with a hint of the Warm Brown mixture. Let dry.

12 Highlight the Birds

Apply and blend the birds' highlights one section at a time, making each stroke follow the direction of the feathers. Moisten each section with Clearblend. Then create a marbleized mixture of Whiteblend, Titanium White and the Cream mixture for the highlights. Apply the highlights with the no. 2 liner. Gradually blend the inside edges of the wet highlights into the shadowed area with the no. 2 round. If a highlight does not blend easily, moisten the no. 2 round with Clearblend. Highlight the wings by starting at the outside tip of the primary feathers, pulling in toward the shadow.

13 *Paint the Ground Mist*

Apply then blend one small section of the mist at a time. Load Clearblend on the no. 2 fan and moisten the water and foliage. Marbleize a mixture of Whiteblend and a touch of the Barely Pink mixture. Load that mixture onto the corner of a no. 2 fan. Tap dabs of it along the bottom of the foliage and the top of the water. Scumble the marbleized mixture over the foliage with a clean, slightly moist no. 12 bristle flat, creating a drifting mist. Let dry. Repeat if needed.

14 *Add the Grass and Final Details*

Paint the grass clusters in irregular sizes and shapes. Apply the paint more densely at the bottom, moving to thin and wispy at the tips. Paint the root area using the Dark Brown mixture loaded on the ½-inch (12mm) multi-texture brush. Add a few taller, more defined grass blades using the no. 2 liner loaded with the Dark Brown, Warm Brown, and Cream mixtures. Look your painting over and touch up as needed. Sign your name and let dry. Spray your painting with an aerosol acrylic painting varnish, and get prepared because "snow's on the way!"

Nesting Grounds

Nesting Grounds
16" × 20" (41cm × 51cm)

This project is designed to teach the concept of using a range of values, from light pastel colors in the distance to medium values in the middle ground and bold dark values in the foreground.

I did not have to look far to get the subject matter for this project; it surrounds the area where I live. When we moved to Florida twenty-seven years ago, the end of my street looked much like this. We would tootle out the natural waterway in our boat and see hundreds of egrets and herons gracing the marsh and trees en route to the open river.

Egrets and herons are beautiful, graceful and fascinating birds. During their nesting season, many of them grow long feathers or plumes on their backs that span the length of their bodies. Around the early 1900s, the fashion industry's desire for feathers caused the price to soar to more than twice that of gold. These birds were hunted by the thousands in their nesting grounds, leaving their babies and unhatched eggs to die.

In the early 1900s, these beautiful birds were in danger of extinction. Now they are protected by a combined effort of concerned citizens and legislation. They are once again nesting along the southern marshes and waterways. Let's capture them on canvas in their nesting grounds.

Materials

Acrylic Colors Burnt Umber, Cadmium Red Medium, Cadmium Yellow Medium, Cerulean Blue, Dioxazine Purple, Sap Green, Payne's Gray, Raw Sienna, Ultramarine Blue, Yellow Ochre Light

Mediums Clearblend and Whiteblend

Brushes 2-inch (51mm) bristle flat, No. 4 bristle flat, ¼-inch (6mm) sable/synthetic flat, No. 12 bristle round, No. 2 round, No. 2 liner, 1½-inch (38mm) hake or ¾-inch (19mm) mop, ½-inch (12mm) multitexture, ⅜-inch (10mm) sable/synthetic angle, No. 2 fan, Tapered painting knife, Natural sea sponge

Pattern Enlarge the pattern on page 103 166 percent.

Other 16" × 20" (41cm × 51cm) stretched canvas, Aerosol acrylic painting varnish, Black and white transfer paper, Paper towels, Stylus

Color Mixtures

Before you begin, prepare these color mixtures on your palette.

Pale Peach	Whiteblend + a touch of Cadmium Yellow Medium + a speck of Cadmium Red Medium
Pale Yellow	40 parts Whiteblend + 1 part Yellow Ochre Light
Dark Green	1 part Sap Green + 1 part Payne's Gray + 1 part Ultramarine Blue + 1 part Burnt Umber
Deep Teal	6 parts Cerulean Blue + 2 parts Whiteblend + 1 part Dark Green mixture
Olive Green	2 parts Raw Sienna + 1 part Sap Green
Gray-Violet	1 part Payne's Gray + 1 part Cerulean Blue + 1 part Whiteblend + a touch of Dioxazine Purple
Light Blue	3 parts Whiteblend + 1 part Cerulean Blue
Light Blue-Violet	Light Blue mixture + a touch of Payne's Gray + a speck of Dioxazine Purple
Light Gray-Green	8 parts Whiteblend + 2 parts Cerulean Blue + 1 part Dark Green mixture + 1 part Payne's Gray

1 Paint the Sky

Transfer the pattern to the canvas (page 7) using black transfer paper, omitting the birds and the dead foreground trees. Paint the sky with the Pale Peach mixture, stroking horizontally using a 2-inch (51mm) bristle flat. Add Cerulean Blue and a touch of Ultramarine Blue to the corner of the unclean brush and apply horizontal streaks across the top of the sky. Wipe the excess paint from the brush, then blend the bottom of the blue streaks by stroking back and forth horizontally until a gradual transition is achieved.

2 Create the Foreground Water

Paint the Pale Peach mixture over the water area with a clean 2-inch (51mm) bristle flat. Add Cerulean Blue and Ultramarine Blue to the brush and apply a darker value of blue across the bottom of the canvas. Blend, leaving the water a darker value than the sky.

3 Paint the Background Foliage

Saturate a sponge and squeeze out the water so it is moist; then, while the sky is still wet, stipple the most-distant foliage with the Light Blue mixture loaded on a sponge. Lay it across the horizon so that it is irregular in shape and size and approximately 2½ inches (7cm) at its tallest point. Load a soupy mixture of the Light Blue mixture and Clearblend onto the no. 2 liner to paint the tree trunks and limbs. Add palm fronds on the tops of some using the same paint and brush. Using the corner of a no. 2 fan and the same mixture, tap small dabs of foliage on a few trees that do not have palm fronds. Do not apply foliage to all trees.

4 Paint the Middle Foliage

Add the Light Gray-Green mixture and a touch of the Light Blue mixture to the unclean sponge and stipple the shorter middle foliage on the right side of the canvas so it sits on the distant water line. Add more of the Light Gray-Green mixture to the unclean sponge, then apply the left side of the distant foliage, making it slightly taller and extending it approximately ½ inch (12mm) lower on the canvas.

5 Add the Distant Water

Use the ⅜-inch (10mm) sable/synthetic angle to apply Whiteblend in the upper-center section of the distant water area. Wipe the excess from the brush, and paint the remainder of the water with the Light Blue mixture. Blend by brushing back and forth with the ½-inch (12mm) multi-texture brush.

6 Create the Marsh Grass

(1) Load the no. 2 fan with the Pale Yellow mixture and paint the top section of the marsh grass. Apply the tips with short, irregular vertical strokes, altering the color occasionally by adding a hint more Whiteblend or Pale Peach mixture. (2) Starting at the foreground marsh water line, make upward strokes using a no. 2 fan loaded with the Dark Green mixture. Establish a dark, dense root area for the grass by applying more pressure at the base of the grass and less pressure as you flip the bristles up. Create stalks (approximately 1 inch [25mm] tall) with wispy tops that connect to the wet pale yellow tips. Reload the brush frequently. (3) Create a gradual transition between the light distant grass and the dark foreground grass by mixing the Dark Green and Pale Yellow mixtures and applying additional ⅛-inch (3mm) choppy vertical strokes randomly through the marsh. Soften the transition of values with short vertical strokes using a clean, dry no. 2 fan or ½-inch (12mm) multitexture brush. Let dry.

7 Apply Grass Reflections

Moisten the the foreground water with Clearblend. Stroke downward from the roots of the dark green grass to create the reflections using the no. 2 fan loaded with the Dark Green mixture. Create additional details on the dark green stalks by stroking vertically along their stems and respective reflections using the ½-inch (12mm) multitexture brush loaded with a soupy mixture of the Light Gray-Green mixture. Let dry.

8 Add the Foreground Foliage and Reflection

Use the tapered painting knife to pile some Dark Green mixture at the base and center of the foreground foliage. Tap over the wet dark green paint with a damp natural sea sponge to create texture and extend the edges into an irregular lacy foliage shape. Add more of the Dark Green mixture to the sponge as needed. Repeat the process underneath the foliage, creating a mirror-image reflection of the shapes above.

9 Highlight the Foreground Foliage

Add the Olive Green mixture to a clean sponge and tap a dull highlight along the top right edges of the bushes and reflections. Add more Raw Sienna to the sponge and tap in the foliage. Sponge-mix and apply several values of yellow-green highlights. Make each highlight lighter by adding more of the Pale Yellow mixture to the Olive Green mixture. Apply these highlights in a progression, with the lightest value on the extreme top and left edges of the foliage, nearest to the light source. Don't cover all the dark green or apply the lightest values in the reflection.

10 Paint the Reflected Light

Using the Deep Teal mixture loaded on a clean sponge, tap reflected light along the left edges of the foliage and the reflection. Add the Gray-Violet mixture to the sponge and tap around in the shadow of the foliage and reflections. Do not cover all the dark green.

11 Apply the Tall Foreground Grass

Load the no. 2 liner with thin paint and add the tall grass at the end of the foliage. Apply a few blades with the Dark Green mixture and any or all the foliage highlight colors. Cross some of the blades to create a natural appearance. Let dry. Transfer the birds and dead tree from the pattern using the white and/or black transfer paper.

12 Paint and Highlight the Foreground Dead Trees

Using the ⅜-inch (10mm) sable/synthetic angle, basecoat the tree scruffily with brush-mixed Burnt Umber and a touch of Ultramarine Blue. Paint each tree and its reflection one at a time, wet-into-wet, turning the brush parallel to the outer edges of each section of the tree. Brush mix and apply the following highlights using short choppy strokes indicating bark with the ½-inch (12mm) multitexture brush. Apply the tan highlight on the top and/or right two-thirds of the trees and reflections using a brush mixture of Burnt Umber and the Pale Peach mixture. Apply highlights on the extreme top and/or right one-third of the trees and reflections using a bright brush mixture of Cadmium Yellow Medium and Cadmium Red Medium. Using the Gray-Violet mixture, paint the reflected light on the extreme left side of the trees and reflections. Let dry.

13 Add the Bromeliads (Air Plants)

Paint the bromeliads using thin paint loaded on the no. 2 liner or no. 2 round. Use the same colors and progression of colors as you used in the foliage. Add seed pod blooms on some stems in the center of the bromeliads with a deep red brush mixture of Cadmium Red Medium and Burnt Umber. Highlight the blooms with Cadmium Red Medium and touch of Cadmium Yellow Medium.

14 Paint and Highlight the Moss

Brush-mix a medium value of gray from Whiteblend, Payne's Gray and a touch of the Light Gray-Green mixture using the ½-inch (12mm) multitexture brush. Hold the brush vertically along the dead tree limb and stroke down, creating various lengths of hanging moss. Turn the brush with a slight swoop to create connecting swags. Tap lightly within the clusters to create density. Lighten the moss color with Whiteblend and highlight the right sides of some clumps.

15 Paint and Highlight the Egrets

Paint the heads, necks and bodies with the Light Blue mixture using the no. 2 liner and no. 2 round. Add the Light Blue-Violet mixture to the shadow of the birds, blending slightly. Let dry. Using the no. 2 liner, apply and immediately blend the highlight on one small section of a bird at a time. Use mostly Whiteblend, slightly marbleized with the Pale Peach and Pale Yellow mixtures. Blend the highlight with a clean no. 2 round moistened with Clearblend. Fade it toward the shadows, where it will gradually disappear. Highlight the top of the heads, necks, backs, wings and tails.

16 *Paint and Highlight the Beaks and Eyes*

Paint the beaks with thinned Yellow Ochre Light. Let dry. Add a bright yellow highlight on the top of each beak with a brush mixture of Cadmium Yellow Medium and White-blend. Use thinned Payne's Gray to paint the legs and add a dot for each eye. Load the no. 2 fan with Clearblend and paint the area below the foreground birds. Using the colors the birds were created with, add squiggly marks to show imperfect reflections of them. Lightly swish back and forth across the reflections using a clean no. 2 fan, distorting the reflections and creating a shimmery effect. Let dry.

17 *Create the Distant Birds*

Double-load the no. 2 liner with the Light Blue-Violet mixture and Whiteblend; paint the illusion of middle and background egrets with tiny dots, dabs and dashes. Make the most-distant birds smaller.

18 *Add the Final Details*

Cover the foreground water, including the reflections, with Clearblend using the ½-inch (12mm) multitexture brush. Alternate the Light Blue mixture with Whiteblend to apply horizontal water lines over the grass, foliage and tree reflections using either the no. 2 liner or the ½-inch (12mm) multitexture brush. Hold the brush horizontally. Diffuse the water lines by lightly stroking over them with a clean multitexture brush moistened with Clearblend. Touch up the birds' legs and any area of your painting as needed. Let dry. Spray your painting with aerosol acrylic painting varnish. Now, armed with your paint, brushes and some great painting techniques, hunt for your favorite birds in their "nesting grounds."

A Special Place

Glazing refers to applying a transparent or translucent layer of paint over a dry layer of paint to change the color. Glazes are often used to strengthen or subdue colors. In this painting you will learn several uses of glazing.

You will use glazing to create atmosphere. You won't directly paint a sky in this composition. The sky is created with successive layers of misty glazes.

Glazing also helps you create depth. In this painting, distance between the trees is developed by applying successive misty glazes over the distant foliage and trees, pushing them back in the composition. Strengthening some of the tree shadows with glazes pulls them forward in the mist.

You will learn to create with glazes glow, sparkle or sunlight on objects. By adding pure white on a couple of foreground trees and rocks then glazing them with a transparent golden glaze, you make them appear to be receiving more direct sunlight than other areas of the painting.

These are only a few of the many uses of glazing. I hope this introduction will enhance your appetite and inspire you to explore more uses for glazing on your own.

A Special Place
20" × 16" (51cm × 41cm)

Materials

Acrylic Colors Burnt Sienna, Burnt Umber, Cadmium Yellow Medium, Dioxazine Purple, Hooker's Green, Payne's Gray, Raw Sienna, Thalo Yellow Green, Titanium White, Ultramarine Blue

Mediums Clearblend and Whiteblend

Brushes 2-inch (51mm) bristle flat, No. 4 bristle flat, ¼-inch (6mm) sable/synthetic flat, No. 2 liner, 1½-inch (38mm) hake or ¾-inch (19mm) mop, ½-inch (12mm) multitexture, ⅜-inch (10mm) sable/synthetic angle, No. 2 fan, Tapered painting knife, Natural sea sponge

Pattern Enlarge the pattern on page 104 188 percent.

Other 20" × 16" (51cm × 41cm) stretched canvas, Aerosol acrylic painting varnish, Black and white transfer paper, Hair dryer, Paper towels, Plastic container to hold glazes, Stylus

Color Mixtures

Before you begin, prepare these color mixtures on your palette. Mix the glazes in a separate container.

Dark Green	1 part Hooker's Green + 1 part Burnt Umber + 1 part Payne's Gray + 1 part Ultramarine Blue
Dark Blue-Green	1 part Ultramarine Blue + 1 part Dark Green mixture
Medium Green	2 parts Dark Green mixture + 1 part Whiteblend
Wheat	2 parts Whiteblend + 1 part Raw Sienna
Warm Tan	2 parts Whiteblend + 1 part Burnt Sienna
Bright Yellow	3 parts Titanium White + 1 part Cadmium Yellow Medium
Medium Blue-Green	1 part Whiteblend + 1 part Dark Blue-Green mixture + 1 part Thalo Yellow Green
Gray-Violet	Whiteblend + a touch each of Payne's Gray, Burnt Umber and Dioxazine Purple
Medium Yellow glaze	24 parts Clearblend + 4 parts water + 1 part Whiteblend + a touch of Cadmium Yellow Medium
Blue-Green glaze	6 parts Clearblend + 1 part water + a touch of Dark Blue-Green mixture
Raw Sienna glaze	6 parts Clearblend + 1 part water + a speck of Raw Sienna

1 Transfer the Design and Paint Trees

Transfer the pattern to the canvas (page 7). With the ⅜-inch (10mm) sable/synthetic angle, basecoat the tree trunk using a brush mixture of Burnt Umber and Payne's Gray. Using thin paint of the same color loaded on the no. 2 liner, apply the limbs on the most-distant trees and outline the water and rocks. Let dry.

2 Detail the Distant Tree Trunks

Load the no. 2 liner with the Wheat mixture, then make choppy strokes to resemble highlighted pieces of bark on the right sides of the trunks. Add Burnt Umber to the no. 2 liner and apply the tan bark through the middle and left side of the tree trunks. Let dry. Apply the underbrush using the Medium Green mixture loaded on the sponge. Tap it densely on the ground and sparsely in the top section. Using less paint and pressure on the sponge, add sparse leaves on the tree limbs.

3 Highlight the Grass

Using a brush mixture of Whiteblend and Cadmium Yellow Medium loaded on the no. 2 fan, stipple highlights along the bottom of the underbrush, creating the crest of the distant mounds of grass. Tap to blend with a clean, dry no. 2 fan.

4 Create the Water

Paint the water with the Dark Blue-Green mixture and a no. 2 fan. Use horizontal strokes in the flat areas and downward arching strokes over the waterfall. Add Whiteblend to the Dark Blue-Green mixture and streak it horizontally through the distant water behind the waterfall. Dry with a hair dryer.

5 Glaze the Canvas

Apply a thin Medium Yellow glaze over the canvas with the 2-inch (51mm) bristle flat or the sponge. Gently blend bold streaks with a clean, dry 1½-inch (38mm) hake or ¾-inch (19mm) mop. Tap the foliage at the base of the center most distant tree with a clean, barely moist sponge to create texture in the wet glaze. Remove some of the glaze from the tree trunks with a clean, moist no. 4 bristle flat or redefine some bark marks on the distant trees, if they do not show through. To redefine the tree trunks, brush-mix a glaze of Clearblend and a touch of Burnt Umber, then apply choppy strokes with a no. 2 liner to create the bark on the lower-left portions of the tree trunks. Add a touch of the Wheat mixture to paint the bark in the center. Add more of the Wheat mixture to the Medium Yellow glaze to paint the bark on the far right.

6 Repaint the Tree Trunks

Repaint the middle ground tree trunk and limbs using a mixture of Burnt Umber and Payne's Gray loaded on the ⅜-inch (10mm) sable/synthetic angle and the no. 2 liner. Highlight the tree bark using the ½-inch (12mm) multi-texture brush or the ⅜-inch (10mm) sable/synthetic angle. Hold the brush vertically and make short, choppy strokes. Use the Warm Tan mixture through the center and the Wheat mixture on the right.

7 Paint the Middle Forest

Using the sponge or the 2-inch (51mm) bristle flat and the Dark Green mixture, paint dense underbrush and grass in the middle ground forest area, connecting it to the water's edge and previous foliage. Tap sparse leaves in the tree. Don't worry about getting the paint on the foreground trees. Add the Medium Blue-Green mixture to create the reflected light in the foliage. Add Thalo Yellow to the same sponge or brush, then tap sparse highlights along the top right sides of some underbrush and foliage clusters. Add a touch of the Wheat mixture and highlight the top right sides of the previous highlight.

8 Create the Second Glaze

Apply a second Medium Yellow glaze over the entire canvas with a 2-inch (51mm) bristle flat or sponge. Blend with the 1½-inch (38mm) hake or the ¾-inch (19mm) mop. Remove some of the glaze from the middle tree with a clean, moist 2-inch (51mm) bristle flat or damp paper towel. Tap the underbrush and ground foliage around and beneath the trees with a clean, moist sponge to remove speckles of the glaze, creating texture and variation in color. Let dry. If the glaze cannot be sufficiently removed from the middle ground tree trunk, brush-mix Clearblend with a touch of Burnt Umber using the ⅜-inch (10mm) sable/synthetic angle or ½-inch (12mm) multitexture brush and tap in the shadow area of the tree trunk. Blot if the color is too dark. Tap a few bark strokes on the right with the Wheat and Warm Tan mixtures in the center.

9 Paint and Highlight the Middle Ground Rocks

Load the ⅜-inch (10mm) sable/synthetic angle with a mixture of Burnt Umber and Payne's Gray. Paint the ground and rocks beside the stream behind the waterfall. Add Whiteblend and Burnt Umber to the paint on the brush and streak dull tan highlights onto a few small rocks.

10 Repaint and Highlight the Trees

Repaint the next two foreground trees and limbs using the ⅜-inch (10mm) sable/synthetic angle and the no. 2 liner, alternating between Burnt Umber and Payne's Gray. Then hold the ½-inch (12mm) multitexture brush vertically to make short, choppy to strokes make the bark highlights and reflected lights on the tree trunks and prominent limbs. Apply the Warm Tan mixture through the center of the tree and the Wheat mixture on the right. Alternate using the Gray-Violet mixture and the Medium Blue-Green mixture mixed with Whiteblend for the the reflected light on the left. Apply choppy strokes of Titanium White in patches on the right side where the brightest sunbeams strike, using a clean ⅜-inch (10mm) sable/synthetic angle. Dry thoroughly with a hair dryer.

11 Glaze the Trees

Apply the Raw Sienna glaze over the trees' highlights. If the glaze is too opaque, or bold. Remove it with a clean moist sponge, then add Clearblend to the Raw Sienna glaze to achieve a translucent glowing glaze.

12 Stipple and Highlight the Foreground Foliage

Using the Dark Green mixture, stipple foliage in the foreground treetops and across the limbs with the no. 2 fan and stipple the underbrush between the foreground rocks and trees with the sponge. Use the Medium Blue-Green mixture to apply reflected light in the center and left side of the foliage. Tap Thalo Yellow Green highlights on the top right of some of the center clusters. Brighten the foliage highlight bordering the left side of the waterfall with the Bright Yellow mixture.

13 Highlight the Grass

Hold the fan horizontally and crunch grass highlights around the rocks and stream using no. 2 Thalo Yellow Green and the Bright Yellow mixture. Let dry. Lightly and sparsely, stipple random leaves around in the uppermost treetops and in the underbrush foliage using the sponge and the Blue-Green glaze. Blot to subdue any leaves that are too bold.

14 Create and Highlight the Waterfall Rocks

Scruffily paint the rocks around the waterfall using the ⅜-inch (10mm) sable/synthetic angle, alternating between Burnt Umber and Payne's Gray. Add the Warm Tan mixture to the same brush, then highlight the tops and right sides of the rocks. Blend slightly between the highlight and shadow with a clean ½-inch (12mm) multitexture brush. Apply the Gray-Violet mixture to create the reflected light along the left side of the rock with a clean ⅜-inch (10mm) sable/synthetic angle; blend the inside edges. Moisten the rocks with Clearblend if the base paint is dry. Apply a small irregular-shaped patch of Titanium White on each of a couple of the rocks at the base of the left tree. Let dry. Apply the Raw Sienna glaze over the dry highlighted portions of the large rocks.

15 Glaze the Foreground Water

Glaze the foreground water with the Blue-Green glaze, using the no. 2 fan. Stoke according to the water movement. With a light blue mixture of Whiteblend and a touch of Ultramarine Blue, stroke horizontally over the Blue-Green glaze, connecting the distant water behind the waterfall to the back edge of the waterfall. Add more Whiteblend to the light blue in the no. 2 fan. Create the spill highlight with downward sloping strokes, curving over the waterfall.

16 Add the Splash

Create the splash by crunching along the bottom of the waterfall using Whiteblend and a touch of Ultramarine Blue loaded on the no. 2 fan. With a clean no. 2 fan, hook onto the bottom of the splash highlight and swish horizontally, connecting it to the foreground water current. Add water ripples in the foremost water with a deeper value made from the Dark Blue-Green mixture and a touch of Whiteblend.

17 Paint the Foreground Tree and Rocks

Paint the leaning tree and rocks in the foreground the same way you painted the rocks in step 14, except the highlight. Highlight them with the Warm Tan mixture, leaving them dull.

18 Add the Limbs

Paint a few limbs crossing the foremost tree on the right using Burnt Umber and the Warm Tan mixture double-loaded on the no. 2 liner.

19 Add the Final Details

Using the ½-inch (12mm) multitexture and the no. 2 liner, pull the lichen and moss down from some middle and foreground limbs. Create reflected light on some of the moss by streaking it with the Gray-Violet and/or Medium Blue-Green mixtures. Sign your name and spray your painting with aerosol acrylic painting varnish. Take a break. Go to "a special place" to enjoy the bountiful beauty of nature.

Twins

Twins
14" × 18" (36cm × 46cm)

No matter where I go, skies and clouds captivate me. From gray, hazy overcast days to bright sunny days filled with an abundance of billowing clouds, we never see two skies alike. I want to paint them all! Old barns and buildings are equally fascinating to me. They make great subjects for paintings. They seem to evoke a feeling of nostalgia in most all of us. Not only do I enjoy painting old buildings from our country, but I also enjoy and appreciate the differences in barns and architecture from other countries.

When a friend from Iceland was showing me photographs from her native country, I was fascinated by the striking likeness of Icelandic barns to barns in the United States. The voluminous clouds in many of her photos also captivated me. Hearing her stories and looking at her photos motivated me to paint. Working from her photographs, with her permission, I created this painting.

This composition is packed with handy techniques that will allow you to create grass, stone and old weathered wood, and special interest is given to the billowing clouds. I hope that after this lesson you will apply these techniques to your future compositions. Maybe you are familiar with some old barns or buildings, or you might already have photos of buildings you would like to paint. If not, start looking around and taking lots of photos. They are a great reference for paintings.

Materials

Acrylic Colors Burnt Sienna, Burnt Umber, Cadmium Red Light, Cadmium Yellow Medium, Dioxazine Purple, Payne's Gray, Sap Green, Vivid Lime Green, Thalo Yellow Green, Titanium White, Ultramarine Blue

Mediums Clearblend and Whiteblend

Brushes 2-inch (51mm) bristle flat, No. 12 bristle round, No. 2 liner, 1½-inch (38mm) hake or ¾-inch (19mm) mop, ½-inch (12mm) multitexture, ⅜-inch (10mm) sable/synthetic angle, No. 2 fan, Tapered painting knife, Natural sea sponge

Pattern Enlarge the pattern on page 105 157 percent.

Other 14" × 18" (36cm × 46cm) stretched canvas, Adhesive-backed paper, Aerosol acrylic painting varnish, Black and white transfer paper, Stylus

Color Mixtures

Before you begin, prepare these color mixtures on your palette.

Bright Yellow	2 parts Whiteblend + 1 part Cadmium Yellow Medium
Dark Green	1 part Sap Green + 1 part Payne's Gray + a touch of Dioxazine Purple
Light Blue	1 part Whiteblend + 1 part Ultramarine Blue + a speck of Dioxazine Purple
Peach	Whiteblend + 1 part Cadmium Red Light
Rust	3 parts Burnt Sienna + a touch of Cadmium Red Light
Dark Brown Shadow	Burnt Umber + Payne's Gray + a touch of Dioxazine Purple
Blue-Green	Ultramarine Blue + 1 part Dark Green mixture + a touch of Titanium White
Medium Green	Dark Green mixture + Vivid Lime Green
Violet-Gray	1 part Peach mixture + 1 part Payne's Gray + a touch of Cadmium Red Light

1 Paint the Background Sky

Transfer the pattern to the canvas (page 7), placing the tallest point on the right barn 6¼ inches (16cm) from the top and 7 inches (18cm) from the right. Cover with a design protector (page 7). Paint the bottom two-thirds of the sky with Whiteblend, using a damp 2-inch (51mm) bristle flat. Add the Peach mixture to the same brush and paint streaks throughout the Whiteblend. Add the Light Blue mixture to the brush and paint the remainder of the sky, making the top darkest by adding more Ultramarine Blue. Using the no. 2 fan, randomly add more of the Peach mixture and a few streaks of the Light Blue mixture to the remainder of the sky if needed, blending as you paint. Slightly smooth harsh brush marks or streaks with a clean no. 2 fan or ¾-inch (19mm) mop. Immediately add the shadows.

2 Create the Cloud Shadows

Add the cloud shadows and blend them into the background wet-into-wet. Using the corner of the 2-inch (51mm) flat lightly loaded with the Violet-Gray mixture, erratically scrub to apply the cloud shadows into the wet sky paint using irregular, circular strokes. Extend the large shadows slightly below the rooftops. Quickly blend the shadow bottoms with the no. 12 bristle round. Blend with the ¾-inch (19mm) mop. Let dry.

3 Paint and Highlight the Grassy Knoll and Evergreen Tree

Use the Dark Green mixture and the no. 2 fan to stipple a base for the knoll and the tree, then highlight the top right areas of the grass and tree with the Medium Green mixture. Mix Thalo Yellow Green and a touch of the Bright Yellow mixture, then lightly tap it on the top and right portion of the medium green highlighted areas.

4 Paint and Highlight the Stone Wall

Paint the wall under the knoll using a scruffy application of the Dark Brown Shadow mixture. Randomly apply irregularly shaped rocks on the wall using the Violet-Gray mixture loaded on the ⅜-inch (10mm) sable/synthetic angle. Let dry. If needed, re-wet the stone wall with Clearblend and add highlights or shadows.

5 Highlight the Clouds

Create a marbleized mixture of Whiteblend and the Peach mixture for the cloud's highlight. Build a soft billowing appearance by working one small puff at a time. Paint a few dabs of the highlight on the top right side of a cloud using the corner of the no. 2 fan, then immediately blend the colors using a tapping or patting motion with the side of the no. 12 bristle round moistened with Clearblend. Blend the inside portion of the wet highlight by picking up highlight paint then tapping randomly to disperse it around on the inside of the cloud until it disappears into the shadow areas. Skip spaces between taps to create the puffy spots. Repeat, making irregular-sized and-shaped connecting puffs. Place the puffs in front of and beside others. Let dry.

6 Add Volume to the Large Cloud Mass

Using the same marbleized mixture as in step 5, apply dabs of highlight in the center area of the largest cloud using a no. 2 fan. Tap and scumble the highlight to blend. Using a Clearblend-moistened no. 12 bristle round, gradually disperse the outer portions of the highlighted area in all directions. This creates a large highlighted portion of the cloud that appears to billow forward, just above the barns.

7 Paint the Barn Roofs

Remove the design protector. Apply Clearblend along the bottom of the roof. Paint the roof using the ⅜-inch (10mm) sable/synthetic angle loaded with the Rust mixture, stroking the paint from top to bottom, parallel to the slant of the roof and overlapping the wet Clearblend. Add a few darker streaks in the rust area with the ½-inch (12mm) multitexture brush and a soupy mixture of Burnt Umber and the Rust mixture, continuing to follow the slope of the roof. Repeat for the smaller roof. Let dry. Moisten the roof areas with Clearblend and reapply paint if needed.

8 Paint the Windows and Garage Opening

Using the ⅜-inch (10mm) sable/synthetic angle, mix and apply the Dark Brown Shadow mixture and Burnt Umber inside the barns' windows, between the barns and inside the barn's garage opening. Add Clearblend to the paint in the center and along the ground to create a glow in the garage. Let dry.

9 Paint the Barn's Wood Grain

Apply the base color, then highlight one section of the barn at a time working wet-into-wet. Apply the base coat with the Dark Brown Shadow mixture to a section of the barn, using the ⅜-inch (10mm) sable/synthetic angle. Alternate applying vertical streaks of the Violet-Gray and Light Blue mixtures over the wet dark brown base using light strokes of the ½-inch (12mm) multitexture brush. Make each section progressively lighter in value to create the barns' dimensions. Highlight the fronts of both barns and the protruding portion of the barn, located to the left of the garage opening, with the Light Blue, Violet-Gray and Peach mixtures. Let dry.

10 Glaze the Windows

With a mixture of Clearblend and the Light Blue mixture, apply a translucent glaze over the windowpane with the ⅜-inch (10mm) sable/synthetic angle. Let dry. Draw random diagonal lines across the panes using Whiteblend loaded on the no. 2 liner, indicating light reflecting on the glass.

11 Create and Shadow the Moldings

Marbleize the Violet-Gray and Peach mixtures with a touch of Whiteblend, then paint the window, door and roof moldings using the no. 2 liner. Apply the moldings on the side of the barn with a duller value, using only the Violet-Gray mixture and a touch of Whiteblend. Let dry. Load some thin Dark Brown Shadow mixture on the no. 2 liner, then draw shadows underneath and on the left sides of the moldings.

12 Underpaint the Grass

Paint the grass under the barn using the no. 2 fan loaded with the Dark Green mixture. Let dry. Brush-mix and apply the grass blades, reflected light and highlights using the no. 2 fan. Use the finished painting as a guide for color placement. As you lighten the value, apply less grass of that value. Use light, wispy strokes for small blades (about ⅛ inch [3mm] high). For taller blades, hold the brush handle down and the bristles up, and flap against the canvas. Blot the root areas of the wet highlight and reflected light strokes to "plant" the grass blades.

13 Highlight the Grass

Using the no. 2 fan, apply the Blue-Green mixture to both sides and the bottom of the grass area to create the reflected light. Apply the Medium Green mixture and paint highlights throughout the center of the foreground grass, adding more of the Dark Green mixture on the edges of the canvas. Starting at the crest of the hill, apply Vivid Lime Green to the center of the dull medium green highlighted area. Apply a lighter lime green color by mixing Vivid Lime Green and Whiteblend, then use it to highlight the center of the Thalo Yellow Green highlighted area. Add some Peach mixture and Whiteblend to the Thalo Yellow Green highlights, then lightly apply a small patch of sunlight at the crest of the hill under the foremost corner of the building.

14 Paint the Flowers

Create a marbleized mixture of Ultramarine Blue and a touch of Whiteblend. Lightly tap a few medium blue patches of flowers in the grass shadows, using the no. 2 fan. Add a touch of Dioxazine Purple to the marbleized blue mixture and apply a few violet flowers.

15 Finishing Touches

Add flying birds using the no. 2 liner loaded with watery Violet-Gray mixture. Sign your name. Let dry. Spray your painting with aerosol acrylic painting varnish to enhance and bring out the glow of this Icelandic beauty.

Bearable

Bearable
14" × 18" (36cm × 46cm)

This painting teaches you to create warmth, both physical and emotional, on a cold white canvas. Nothing brings out warm, fuzzy feelings better than a cuddly teddy bear lit by early morning sun coming through the window. With that in mind, I selected warm colors for the palette.

In this composition, you will get a lot of practice at controlling strong lights and darks, making them work together with soft transitions. You will also learn to use glazes to create the illusion of glass and of sheer lace curtains. Finally, you will learn to create the appearance of contoured, knobby fabric by tapping with your sponge or stippling brush. All are handy techniques to have in your bag of artist tricks!

This teddy bear is more than "bearable," it is adorable and educational. It is designed with many things in mind. It is my hope that it will expand your artistic skills and techniques and leave a warm feeling in your heart as well.

Materials

Acrylic Colors Burnt Sienna, Burnt Umber, Cadmium Red Medium, Cadmium Yellow Medium, Dioxazine Purple, Grumbacher Red, Payne's Gray, Raw Sienna, Titanium White

Mediums Clearblend and Whiteblend

Brushes 2-inch (51mm) bristle flat, No. 4 and 8 bristle flat, ¼-inch (6mm) sable/synthetic flat, No. 12 bristle round, No. 2 liner, 1½-inch (38mm) hake or ¾-inch (19mm) mop, ½-inch (12mm) multitexture, ⅜-inch (10mm) sable/synthetic angle, No. 2 fan, Tapered painting knife, Natural sea sponge

Pattern Enlarge the pattern on page 106 183 percent.

Other 14" × 18" (36cm × 46cm) stretched canvas, Aerosol acrylic painting varnish, Black and white transfer paper, Hair dryer, Plastic container to hold glazes, Stylus

Color Mixtures

Before you begin, prepare these color mixtures on your palette. Mix the glaze in a separate container.

Dark Brown	4 parts Burnt Umber + 1 part Dioxazine Purple + 1 part Payne's Gray
Deep Violet-Gray	4 parts Whiteblend + 2 parts Payne's Gray + 2 parts Dioxazine Purple + 1 part Burnt Umber
Light Yellow	4 parts Titanium White + 1 part Cadmium Yellow Medium
Maroon	2 parts Grumbacher Red + 1 part Burnt Umber
Medium Brown	2 parts Burnt Sienna + 1 part Raw Sienna
Off-White	Titanium White + a touch of Cadmium Yellow Medium
Portrait	Burnt Sienna + a touch of Cadmium Red Medium + a speck Cadmium Yellow Medium + a touch of Titanium White
Rose-Brown	1 part Portrait mixture + 1 part Whiteblend
Rust	3 parts Cadmium Yellow Medium + 1 part Burnt Sienna + a touch of Cadmium Red Medium
Tan-Brown	1 part Medium Brown mixture + 1 part Raw Sienna +1 part Cadmium Yellow Medium + 1 part Whiteblend
Pale Yellow glaze	2 parts water + 2 parts Clearblend + 1 part Whiteblend + a touch of Cadmium Yellow Medium

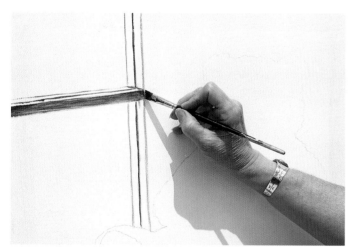

1 Transfer the Design and Outline the Window

Transfer the window and the outline of the teddy bear from the pattern to the canvas (page 7). Use the ¼-inch (6mm) sable/synthetic flat to paint the center of the bear's nose 5¼ inches (13cm) from the top and 11 inches (28cm) from the left. Paint the window sash and draw a line through the outside window moldings with a brush mixture of Burnt Sienna and Burnt Umber. Dry this with a hair dryer.

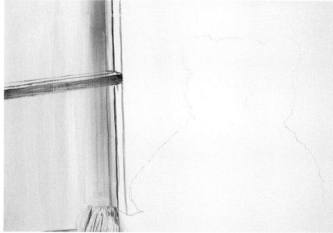

2 Glaze the Window

Apply the translucent Pale Yellow glaze over the window opening and moldings with the 2-inch (51mm) bristle flat. Add a touch of the Medium Brown mixture to the corner of the brush and apply subtle, pastel, warm brown streaks vertically over the wet glaze, placing the most prominent streaks along the right molding. With a no. 2 fan, apply faint random streaks of Whiteblend vertically through the center. Do not paint the window opaquely or cover the entire glaze with the streaks. Blend slightly and let dry.

3 Retouch and Shadow the Moldings

Retouch the window moldings and sash using the ⅜-inch (10mm) sable/synthetic angle and the no. 2 liner with a mixture of Burnt Umber and Burnt Sienna, and highlight with the Off-White mixture. Add the sash shadow using watery Dark Brown mixture.

4 Basecoat and Retransfer the Bear

Apply a scruffy basecoating on the teddy bear and the shadow area behind him by scumbling with a double-loaded no. 8 bristle flat. Use Burnt Umber in the darkest areas, and add Burnt Sienna to the Burnt Umber to paint the lightest areas. Let dry. Realign the pattern and transfer the bear and its detail with white transfer paper.

5 Paint the Face

Basecoat the eyes, the nose, the seam under the nose, and a big smile using the ⅜-inch (10mm) sable/synthetic angle and the no. 2 liner loaded with creamy Payne's Gray. Let dry.

6 Scumble the Wall

Using the no. 8 bristle flat or ⅜-inch (10mm) sable/synthetic angle, scumble a progression of colors on the wall between the window and bear. Apply the Rust mixture closest to the window. Randomly add Cadmium Yellow Medium, the Portrait mixture, Burnt Sienna and Burnt Umber as you paint away from the window, darkening the color as you move away from the light and overlapping the previously painted shadow area. Blend slightly with short erratic stokes of a clean, dry ¾-inch (19mm) mop.

7 Paint the Windowsill

Using horizontal strokes from a clean ⅜-inch (10mm) sable/synthetic angle, paint the Rust mixture next to the window and in front of the bear's right foot. Create a defined shadow in the bottom left corner and to the right of the legs with the Dark Brown mixture. Blend slightly with a clean, dry 2-inch (51mm) bristle flat or no. 2 fan. Complete the final blending with a clean, dry ¾-inch (19mm) mop. Paint a shimmer of light along the edge of the sill behind the bear with the ⅜-inch (10mm) sable/synthetic angle and a brush mixture of Burnt Sienna and a touch of Whiteblend. Blend the inside edge with a clean 2-inch (51mm) bristle flat slightly moistened with Clearblend. Blend with a clean, dry ¾-inch (19mm) mop.

8 Create and Detail the Curtain

Apply clean tap water on the wall and top of the bear's head and left shoulder with a sponge. Lightly load a small section of the sponge with the Pale Yellow glaze and Whiteblend. Tap the palette to blend the colors, then apply swooping, translucent streaks on the wall to create a sheer curtain. Quickly remove any excess paint from the wall and bear with a clean section of the sponge. For a sheerer curtain, remove excess paint. Add Whiteblend to the Pale Yellow glaze in the sponge and streak off-white sheers along the left side of the canvas. Add the Rust mixture to the same sponge and tap the palette to blend, then apply shadow streaks in the sheer curtains. Randomly and lightly tap around on the sheers to create the illusion of embroidery. Let dry.

9 Create a Speckled Texture on the Bear

Softly tap the bear's shadow, highlight and reflected light colors using a lightly loaded portion of the sponge, no. 2 fan, or ½-inch (12mm) multitexture brush. Paint one section at a time. Use the Dark Brown mixture to apply shadows on the bottom and back of the body, arms, legs, head, muzzle; around the chin and neck; and inside the ears and eye sockets with the sponge. Tap to blend toward the inside or light in each area. To maintain the texture yet create a gradual transition, tap back and forth where the colors merge with a clean portion of the sponge or blot with your finger.

10 Highlight the Bear

Create highlight colors that span from dull to very light. Starting at the inside edge of the shadows, use the Medium Brown mixture to speckle the remaining sections with highlights. Add the Rose-Brown mixture to the sponge and tap it along the left side of the bear's left arm and along the top of the bear's left leg. Sparsely tap the remaining sunlit parts of the bear with the Medium Brown and Rose-Brown mixtures. Tap and blot to blend.

Using the Tan-Brown mixture, tap to apply then to blend highlights along the top left side of the bear using the sponge. Let dry. Gradually lighten the value by adding Whiteblend in increments and repeat, applying at least two additional, progressively lighter values of tan highlights. Tap to highlight and blend the bear's ears using the no. 2 fan.

11 *Highlight the Ears and Add the Brightest Highlights*

Frame the inner ears by tapping Burnt Sienna on the right ridge edges and the Rose-Brown mixture on the left ridge edges. Blot to blend. Let dry. Use the no. 2 fan or ½-inch (12mm) multitexture brush to sparingly tap the Light Yellow mixture in the lightest areas on the ears, head, arms, legs, top of the muzzle, chin and mouth. Tap or blot to blend. Let dry. Lightly and more sparingly tap the Off-White mixture on the ear, muzzle, arm and leg nearest the window with the no. 2 fan or ½-inch (12mm) multitexture brush. Tap or blot to blend. Let dry.

12 *Add Reflected Light*

Using the Deep Violet-Gray mixture, tap to apply and to blend reflected light along the right side of the bear's head, ears, muzzle, arms, legs and body using the no. 2 fan.

13 Finish the Bear's Face

Paint and blend the eyes and nose using the ⅜-inch (10mm) sable/synthetic angle and no. 4 bristle flat. Apply Payne's Gray on the outer portions and the Deep Violet-Gray mixture in the centers; blend, creating a convex appearance. Let dry. Add catchlights to the eyes and nose using Whiteblend loaded on the no. 2 liner. Connect the mouth and nose using watery Payne's Gray loaded on the no. 2 liner.

14 Detail the Feet

Paint and blend the bottom of the feet smoothly using the ⅜-inch (10mm) sable/synthetic angle. Use the Portrait mixture for the lightest value, Burnt Sienna for the middle value and Burnt Umber for the darkest. Blend with a clean ⅜-inch (10mm) sable/synthetic angle.

15 Add the Finishing Touches

Apply the ribbon and bow using a no. 2 liner loaded with the Maroon mixture. Highlight it with a mixture of Cadmium Red Medium, Cadmium Yellow Light and a touch of Whiteblend. Let dry. Remove any unpainted pattern lines with a clean, moist sponge.

If the bear is too bright, tone down the bear with a glaze mixture of Clearblend and any of the bear's colors for the area. Tap with a clean, moist sponge to blend and remove excess glaze. Sign your name. Spray your painting with aerosol acrylic painting varnish to bring out the radiant glow. Give yourself a big bear hug!

Wonders of the Deep

Underwater scenes are daunting to many budding artists. The mystery of how to accomplish a realistic scene is as obscure as what is hidden below the water's surface. This doesn't have to be true for you.

In this composition, you will learn that by using a thin glaze you can easily simulate light rays penetrating the water's surface—creating the illusion of being underwater. Even if underwater scenes are not your favorites, these techniques are also useful for landscapes. By changing the colors and composition, you can use this same technique to show strong rays illuminating objects above ground, as well.

Painting underwater objects doesn't need to be intimidating either. Creating the illusion of a multicolored coral reef is easily accomplished by stippling with a lacy-edged natural sea sponge. Larger fish are easily created by first establishing their shapes then adding the details. Schools of sea life—squid and fish—can be suggested with a multitude of short brushstrokes.

Even the diver is a snap to paint. By using various values of one color and a few contrasting dabs of paint, you can magically bring him to life. You can almost hear the bubbles as he breathes.

Now let's go explore the "wonders of the deep."

Wonders of the Deep
20" × 16" (51cm × 41cm)

Materials

Acrylic Colors Cadmium Yellow Medium, Cerulean Blue Dioxazine Purple, Payne's Gray, Thalo Crimson, Thalo Green, Titanium White, Ultramarine Blue

Mediums Clearblend, Slowblend, Whiteblend

Brushes 2-inch (51mm) bristle flat, No. 8 bristle flat, ¼-inch (6mm) sable/synthetic flat, No. 2 round, No. 2 liner, 1½-inch (38mm) hake or ¾-inch (19mm) mop, ½-inch (12mm) multi-texture, ⅜-inch (10mm) sable/synthetic angle, No. 2 fan, Tapered painting knife, Natural sea sponge

Pattern Enlarge the pattern on page 107 200 percent.

Other 20" × 16" (51cm × 41cm) stretched canvas, Aerosol acrylic panting varnish, Black and white transfer paper, Plastic container to hold glazes, Stylus

Color Mixtures

Before you begin, prepare these color mixtures on your palette. Mix the glaze in a separate container.

Prussian Blue	10 parts Ultramarine Blue + 1 part Thalo Green + 1 part Payne's Gray
Dark Blue	3 parts Payne's Gray + 3 parts Dioxazine Purple + 1 part Prussian Blue mixture + 1part Thalo Green
Medium Blue	Prussian Blue mixture + various amounts of Whiteblend (to create different values)
Violet-Gray	2 parts Whiteblend + 1 part Payne's Gray + a touch of Dioxazine Purple
Light Violet-Gray	1 part Violet-Gray mixture + 1 part Whiteblend + a touch of Dioxazine Purple
Light Blue	marbleize 1 part Cerulean Blue + 1 part Whiteblend
Bright Yellow	2 parts Whiteblend + 1 part Cadmium Yellow Medium
Light Yellow	Bright Yellow mixture + a touch of Clearblend
Orange	marbleize 1 part Thalo Crimson + 1 part Cadmium Yellow Medium + 1 part Whiteblend
Pink	marbleize 2 parts Whiteblend + 1 part Thalo Crimson
Turquoise	marbleize 2 parts Whiteblend + 1 part Thalo Green
Prussian Blue glaze	3 parts Clearblend + 1 part Slowblend + a touch of the Prussian Blue mixture + 1 part water

1 Transfer and Paint the Diver

Transfer the diver and reef outlines from the pattern (page 7) using black transfer paper, placing the diver approximately 5½ inches (14cm) from the top and 6 inches (15cm) from the left. Paint the diver using the Violet-Gray mixture and the ⅜-inch (10mm) sable/synthetic angle, no. 2 liner and any other small brush of your choice. Add a touch of Whiteblend to the Violet-Gray mixture and paint the mask, forward arm and hand, blending where the arm and shoulder meet.

2 Create the Distant Reef

Paint a rough and ragged distant reef using the no. 2 fan loaded with the Violet-Gray mixture. Scumble erratically to create irregular textures and shapes.

4 Create the Light Rays

Using the 2-inch (51mm) bristle flat or a sponge, apply the light rays with the Prussian Blue glaze. Apply the glaze by stroking from the top left corner to the bottom right corner, crossing over the diver and reef. Fan out the subsequent strokes, but don't bend or curve any of them. Immediately remove some of the glaze with a clean, moist sponge to create light beams or bolder rays if needed. Lightly blend with the ¾-inch (19mm) mop or 1½-inch (38mm) hake if needed, stroking in the direction of the beams. Let dry. Repeat if the painting is too pale.

3 Paint the Foreground and Reef Base

Working one small section at a time, stipple the foreground using the Dark Blue mixture on a 2-inch (51mm) bristle flat, slightly overlapping the bottom edges of the distant reef. Immediately tap the edges with a damp sponge to create soft lacy edges. Sponge-mix the Prussian Blue mixture and Whiteblend, then tap along the top edge and randomly throughout the foreground reef creating the reflected light. Apply sparingly in the bottom corners. Create twigs and seaweed along the reef's edges using thinned Violet-Gray and Prussian Blue mixtures loaded onto a no. 2 liner. Let dry.

5 Paint and Highlight the Schools of Fish

Paint the suggestion of various-sized distant squid and other sea life using the Medium Blue mixture loaded on the no. 2 liner. Add some of the Dark Blue mixture to darken the paint mixture for some middle ground fish. For some schools, double-load the brush with the Pink mixture and Whiteblend. Rotate the brush, putting the pink on the bottom of some fish and on the top of other schools. Let dry. Highlight the bottoms of a few large, middle ground fish with the Pink mixture and blend the inside edge over the bottom of the fish.

6 Underpaint the Angelfish

Individually paint the foreground fish, alternating between a ⅜-inch (10mm) sable/synthetic angle, no. 2 liner, no. 2 round and ¼-inch (6mm) sable/synthetic flat. Paint a base-coat on the angelfish using the Light Violet-Gray mixture loaded on the ¼-inch (6mm) sable/synthetic flat. Add White-blend to the belly, and blend to create a convex shape. Let dry. Moisten the fish with Clearblend, then highlight the top of the fish and fin using a no. 2 liner loaded with White-blend and a touch of the Pink mixture. Sightly blend the inside edge. Use the Violet-Gray mixture to apply a shadow along the bottom of the fish and blend. Let dry.

7 Detail the Angelfish

Apply the Bright Yellow mixture on the tail of the angelfish with a ¼-inch (6mm) sable/synthetic flat. Slightly blend the inside edge over the back end of the fish. Add spines to the tail fin with the no. 2 liner loaded with Whiteblend. Paint a dark eye patch on each angelfish and irregular stripes across their bodies using Payne's Gray loaded on the ¼-inch (6mm) sable/synthetic flat. Use the Bright Yellow mixture to add a dot in each eye patch for the eye. Let dry. Paint a side fin across the center of the fish with thin Violet-Gray mixture. Let dry and highlight with thinned Light Yellow mixture. Paint the mouths with a clean no. 2 liner loaded with watery Payne's Gray. For some distant angelfish, add a touch of the Light Violet-Gray mixture to each detail color for a distant appearance.

8 Paint the Butterfly Fish

Paint the body of the butterfly fish with the Orange mixture; highlight the top and front with the Light Yellow mixture and blend. Paint the fins with the Light Yellow mixture. Randomly streak the Orange mixture over the fins. Use the Light Yellow mixture to add spines on the top fins. Add a Payne's Gray eye patch with a dot of the Bright Yellow mixture for the eye.

9 Paint the Pink Coral

Using a sponge, lightly tap patches of brightly colored coral throughout the foreground reef. Lighten each coral color with Whiteblend for its highlight and tap it on the top left sides of the patches. Start by using the Pink mixture to apply and highlight the pink coral, placing small patches randomly throughout the reef with predominate patches between the foreground fish. Add Dioxazine Purple to the paint on the sponge, then lightly tap along the right sides of the pink clusters, creating shadows. Using the Violet-Gray mixture, add coral stipples around the bottom and corners of the canvas. Add the Light Blue mixture to the paint on the sponge and randomly tap blue coral in a few void areas. With a clean sponge and the Turquoise mixture, add and highlight coral patches. Sparingly, use the Orange mixture to add and highlight orange coral in the same manner.

10 Add Tips to the Coral

Apply a few tips with the ¼-inch (6mm) sable/synthetic flat and the coral colors lightened with a touch of Titanium White. Let dry.

11 Create the Bubbles

With the no. 2 fan and the Medium Blue mixture, apply bubbles coming from the diver's mask. Smudge the wet paint in a squiggle motion with a clean brush or your finger, fading the bubbles as they trail away from the diver.

12 *Highlight the Bubbles*

Apply random Whiteblend dabs along the medium blue bubbles and smudge as before. Dip the point of the no. 2 liner—or the brush handle—in Whiteblend, then randomly tap bubbles of various sizes and shapes. Let dry.

13 *Add the Final Details*

Double-load a liner with watery Dark Blue, Pink and Light Yellow mixtures; apply dark twigs across the reef and the diver's feet. Sign your painting. Let it dry. Spray with aerosol acrylic painting varnish and go diving for sunken treasures in the "wonders of the deep."

Last Light of Day

Last Light of Day
16" × 20" (41cm × 51cm)

A symbol of the family farm, barns like this once spanned the United States. In its heyday, this particular barn stood proudly along the Appalachian Trail in North Carolina, serving many families for many years. Then this barn saw its "last light of day." It succumbed to urban expansion and tourism construction now known as the Blue Ridge Parkway.

We can immortalize our heritage through art by painting nostalgic scenes that are physically disappearing.

This is crucial because they are disappearing more rapidly now than during any other period in our history.

This project is designed to rekindle and savor the laid-back, cozy feeling of life on the farm that is coveted by many seeking a simpler, stress-free lifestyle. The techniques used to create this scene are like the scene itself, easygoing and simple.

Materials

Acrylic Colors Burnt Sienna, Burnt Umber, Cadmium Yellow Medium, Dioxazine Purple, Payne's Gray, Thalo Crimson, Titanium White

Mediums Clearblend, Whiteblend

Brushes 2-inch (51mm) bristle flat, No. 8 bristle flat, ¼-inch (6mm) sable/synthetic flat, No. 12 bristle round, No. 2 round, No. 2 liner, 1½-inch (38mm) hake or ¾-inch (19mm) mop, ½-inch (12mm) multitexture, ⅜-inch (10mm) sable/synthetic angle, No. 2 fan, Tapered painting knife, Natural sea sponge

Pattern Enlarge the pattern on page 108 155 percent.

Other 16" × 20" (41cm × 51cm) stretched canvas, Aerosol acrylic painting varnish, Adhesive-backed paper, Paper towels, Stylus, White transfer paper

Color Mixtures

Before you begin, prepare these color mixtures on your palette.

Dark Brown	3 parts Burnt Umber + 2 parts Payne's Gray + 1 part Dioxazine Purple
Medium Gray	8 parts Payne's Gray + 4 parts Whiteblend + 1 part Thalo Crimson
Dusty Peach	30 parts Whiteblend + 1 part Medium Gray mixture + 2 parts Cadmium Yellow Medium + 1 part Thalo Crimson
Violet-Gray	3 parts Whiteblend + 2 parts Payne's Gray + 1 part Dioxazine Purple
Pinkish-Violet	10 parts Whiteblend + 2 parts Payne's Gray + 1 part Dioxazine Purple
Light Gray	1 part Medium Gray mixture + 1 part Whiteblend

1 Paint and Blend the Sky and Treetops

Basecoat the canvas with the Medium Gray mixture using a 2-inch (51mm) bristle flat or sponge. Let dry. Transfer the pattern (page 7), placing the roof's front peak 6 inches (15cm) from the top and 10 inches (25cm) from the left. Cover the barn with a design protector (page 7).

Apply a fifty-fifty mixture of water and Clearblend to the area where treetops will be, using a 2-inch (51mm) bristle flat. Paint an irregular-shaped sky using the Dusty Peach mixture with the 2-inch (51mm) bristle flat, overlapping the wet Clearblend. Create leafy treetops by tapping to lift off some of the wet sky, then paint along the bottom of the sky using a clean, moist sponge. Tap the lifted paint over the forest area to create additional treetops and irregular foliage shapes. Using the residue in the sponge, tap foliage and texture in the lower forest behind the barn. Lightly blend the sky with the 1½-inch (38mm) hake or ¾-inch (19mm) mop using erratic strokes. If needed, add the Violet-Gray mixture to the paint on the sponge and create more defined treetops.

2 Shadow the Forest

Load a mixture of Payne's Gray and Clearblend on the no. 2 fan and apply a shadow at the base of the forest, working on one side of the barn at a time. Smack the brush flat against the canvas. Texture the shadow by tapping over the wet paint with a clean, moist sponge. Tap heavily along the top of the shadows to blend and develop a gradual transition. If the shadow becomes too dark or develops hard lines, add the Medium Gray mixture to the sponge and tap lightly to correct the appearance.

3 Redefine and Accent the Treetops

Redefine the treetops by tapping lightly using the Dusty Peach mixture loaded on the moist sponge. Add the Pinkish-Violet mixture to the sponge, then lightly stipple accents in the treetops, extending to the most distant tree-tops. Overlap the sky slightly. Blend and create a gradual color transition by lightly tapping along the bottom edge of the wet paint using the clean, moist part of a sponge.

4 Establish and Highlight the Hillside

Lightly tap accents sparingly over the entire hillside with the Pinkish-Violet mixture on a sponge. Tap lightly over the hillside again using a clean sponge sparsely loaded with the Light Gray mixture. Apply more paint along the crest of the hill in the center and progressively less toward the bottom and sides of the canvas. Tap over the wet paint with the clean part of the sponge to create a softer look. This blends, softens and gradually disperses the paint. Mix equal amounts of Whiteblend and the Light Gray mixture to high-light the center portion of the previous area that you high-lighted with the Light Gray mixture. Tap to blend the edges.

5 Shadow the Hillside

Add a touch of Dioxazine Purple to darken and make the Medium Gray mixture slightly more violet. Lightly tap this color in the bottom corners with the sponge to create shadowy areas. Apply less shadow color as you sponge up and into the center. Tap to blend the inside portions of the shadow areas using a clean portion of the sponge. Let dry. Remove the design protector.

6 Paint the Barn

Use the ⅜-inch (10mm) sable/synthetic angle, ½-inch (12mm) multitexture brush and no. 2 liner to paint and blend the barn. Paint the windows, doors, holes in the barn and spaces between the two sections of the tin roof with the Dark Brown mixture loaded on the ¼-inch (6mm) sable/synthetic flat. Paint the left side of the silo with the Dark Brown mixture and the right side with Burnt Sienna and blend the colors. Brush-mix Whiteblend and Burnt Sienna, then blend this mixture into the center of the wet Burnt Sienna on the silo. Paint the inner portion with the Dark Brown mixture and blend. Apply Burnt Sienna on the outer por-tion of the "curled tin." Let dry.

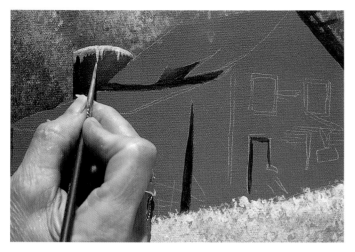

7 Paint the Snow on the Silo

Using the no. 2 liner, apply the snow on top of the silo with the Violet-Gray mixture; then highlight it with Whiteblend, using more highlight on the right side. Pull down a few icicles. Let dry.

8 Apply and Blend the Roof

Work on one section of the roof at a time, making the brushstrokes according to the angle of each section. With the ⅜-inch (10mm) sable/synthetic angle and the Violet-Gray mixture, apply streaks in the lower portions of each roof section and Whiteblend streaks down from the top (don't cover the entire base) overlapping the edges of the violet-gray. Blend where they overlap with the ½-inch (12mm) multitexture brush. Let dry. Apply a broken line of Whiteblend on the leading edge of the right roof and on a few broken slats using the no. 2 liner.

9 Paint and Highlight the Barn

Basecoat each section of the barn using the ⅜-inch (10mm) sable/synthetic angle with a mixture of Clearblend and the Dark Brown mixture. Using the ½-inch (12mm) multitexture brush and vertical strokes, highlight the wet, basecoated section of the barn with both the Medium Gray and Violet-Gray mixtures. Repeat for each section, applying an additional Dusty Peach mixture highlight on the front of the barn, changing the center highlight streaks to horizontal. Let dry.

10 *Detail the Barn*

If needed, use white transfer paper to reestablish the barn details. With the no. 2 liner and ⅜-inch (10mm) sable/synthetic angle, touch up and/or paint the eaves, cracks and hayloft openings with the Dark Brown mixture. Paint the door with the Dark Brown mixture using the ⅜-inch (10mm) sable/synthetic angle, then apply soft vertical streaks of the Violet-Gray mixture with the ½-inch (12mm) multitexture brush. Apply the moldings, slats, broken boards and fence on the front of the barn using a marbleized mixture of the Dusty Peach mixture and a touch of the Dark Brown mixture loaded on the no. 2 liner—use the Violet-Gray mixture for those on the left side of the barn. Add faint shadows underneath and on the left of the moldings using the no. 2 liner loaded with watery Dark Brown mixture.

11 *Paint the Hay*

Using the ¼-inch (6mm) flat or ½-inch (12mm) multitexture, brush-mix Cadmium Yellow Medium, Burnt Sienna and a touch of Whiteblend, creating a dull straw color. Use the mixture to tap hay in the openings of the barn loft. Add a touch more Cadmium Yellow Medium and Whiteblend to create a light straw color and tap highlights on the top area of the hay piles.

12 *Stipple the Bushes*

Load a brush mixture of Payne's Gray and Clearblend on a no. 8 bristle flat and stipple bushes on the left side of the barn. Lightly stipple a frosty highlight on the tops of the bushes with the no. 8 bristle flat and a mixture of the Violet-Gray mixture and a touch of the Dusty Peach mixture. Paint the rocks, hay piles and any other items around the barn using the ⅜-inch (10mm) sable/synthetic angle alternating between the Dark Brown mixture, Burnt Sienna and the straw color. Blot their bottoms to blend them into the grass. Pile snow on top of a few objects using the Violet-Gray mixture and Whiteblend loaded on the no. 2 liner or ⅜-inch (10mm) sable/synthetic angle.

13 Paint the Tree Trunks

Add tree trunks to some of the dark foliage using the no. 2 liner double-loaded with the Dark Brown and Violet-Gray and/or Dusty Peach mixtures. Use the Dark Brown mixture double-loaded with Whiteblend for the tree in front of the barn, pulling it forward into the painting. Double-load the no. 2 liner with the Violet-Gray mixture and Whiteblend and paint the rickety fence. Using the no. 2 fan, lightly tap a faint shadow at the base of the foremost tree with the Violet-Gray mixture. Make sure it follows the contour of the hillside. Blot to subdue the shadow if it is too bold.

14 Add the Final Details

Anchor the barn and area surrounding it by lightly crunching snow-covered grass at their base using the no. 2 fan loaded with Whiteblend and a speck of the Dusty Peach mixture. Tap to blend the root area, as needed, with a clean, damp sponge or a no. 2 fan brush. Let dry. Spray your painting with acrylic aerosol painting varnish. Enjoy the "last light of day."

Southern Beauty

Southern Beauty
16" × 20" (44cm × 51cm)

Acrylics work great on traditional watercolor surfaces. They can be watered down and used in the same manner as transparent watercolors or applied more heavily to give the appearance of gouache. In my opinion, the major differences between watercolors and acrylics are that the (1) acrylics keep their brilliance and do not fade when they dry and (2) will not reactivate or spread again if they are remoistened. These qualities even entice some accomplished watercolorists to use acrylics as their primary medium or to at least include acrylics with the watercolors on their palettes.

Like watercolors, acrylics can be applied beautifully on either hot- or cold-pressed watercolor paper. For this demonstration, I did not use watercolor paper. I chose to use Crescent 300-lb. (640 gsm) illustration board. Illustration board is extremely convenient and economical and is a fun surface for this "watercolor" technique. It requires no preparation and stands rigidly on an easel.

Acrylics can be substituted for watercolors to paint any subject or in any style of painting from photographic realism to loose abstracts. For variety, it is fun to mix different styles in the same composition. This "southern beauty" will allow you to experience some of that.

Materials

Acrylic Colors Burnt Sienna, Burnt Umber, Cadmium Yellow Medium, Dioxazine Purple, Payne's Gray, Sap Green, Thalo Crimson, Ultramarine Blue

Brushes No. 2 liner, 1½-inch (38mm) hake or ¾-inch (19mm) mop, ½-inch (12mm) multitexture, ⅜-inch (10mm) sable/synthetic angle, No. 2 fan, Tapered painting knife, Natural sea sponge

Pattern Enlarge the pattern on page 109 154 percent.

Other 16" x 20" (41cm x 51cm) 300-lb. (640gsm) illustration board, Bubble watercolor palette, Black transfer paper, Cotton swabs, Incredible Nib (or an old brush for applying liquid frisket), Liquid frisket, Liquid soap, Stylus

Color Mixtures

Before you begin, prepare these color mixtures on your palette.

Blue-Green	2 parts Ultramarine Blue + 1 part Sap Green
Dusty Rose	1 part Thalo Crimson + 1 part Payne's Gray
Dusty Purple	1 part Dioxazine Purple + 1 part Payne's Gray
Maroon	2 parts Burnt Umber + 1 part Dioxazine Purple
Navy	1 part Ultramarine Blue + 1 part Payne's Gray

Using the Bubble Watercolor Palette

Place a pea-size dollop of Burnt Umber, Burnt Sienna, Cadmium Yellow Medium and each color mixture above in its own well. Fill each well half-full of water and agitate the edge of the paint, dissolving it into the water. If you have this type palette, prepare the center portion as you would a wet palette, or prepare a separate wet palette for mixing colors.

No white paint is used in this painting. The white is the surface of the paper. The color values are controlled by the amount of water added to the paint. To lighten a color, add more water, allowing more of the white surface to show. When one application is dry, it is easy to darken areas by adding layers or washes. Before starting your painting, test the opacity of each color on a scrap piece of the painting surface.

Paint, then immediately "wash out" to blend one small section of the painting at a time. In each section, apply clean water where the blend or color transition will occur. Apply the paint so that it overlaps the edge of the wet area, then direct the flow of color with a clean, wet brush. Avoid unwanted hard edges and sharp lines by applying enough paint and water. If a hard edge appears, remove it immediately with a cotton swab. Practice on a scrap of the surface you're working on to perfect the technique. Also practice on the scrap when you change the consistency of paint to strengthen or lighten colors.

1 Mask Out the Flower

Transfer the pattern to the illustration board (page 7), placing the flower left of center. Use a brush or the Incredible Nib to apply the liquid frisket. Before dipping the brush or nib into the frisket, wet it, then saturate it with liquid soap, then wipe it away. This creates a barrier so the frisket can be easily removed from its application tool. Apply the frisket along the inside edges of the petals, stamen, leaves and stems. Immediately wash your nib or brush with soap and water, removing all residue. Let dry.

2 Apply the Background Colors

Starting about 1 inch (25mm) below the bottom of the sketch, sponge clean water down and outward. Alternate randomly using the Maroon, Dusty Rose, Navy and occasionally Blue-Green and Dusty Purple mixtures. Paint one small section at a time using the ⅜-inch (10mm) sable/synthetic angle, overlapping into the wet area. Create drips and runs and direct the dispersion of colors away from the leaves and flowers with a no. 2 fan or mop. While wet, remove excess paint, drips and runs with a clean, damp ¾-inch (19mm) sponge.

3 Add More Colors Around the Flower

Continue adding colors around the flower, turning the surface so the drips and runs move away from the flower. Turn it completely upside down for the top area. Let dry. Add more paint to darken the bottom area. Elongate the runs by adding water to create runs and drips, directing the flow with the no. 2 fan. Darken other areas, if needed, in the same manner. Let dry.

4 Paint the Magnolia Petals

Remove the frisket on the stems and leaves by rubbing the edges, lifting and rolling the dried frisket into a ball. Paint the background between the magnolia petals using the no. 2 liner and the background colors.

5 Paint the Stems

Moisten the top and/or right sides of a section of a stem with the ½-inch (12mm) multitexture brush and clean water. Apply Burnt Umber to the left side and/or bottom of the stem, overlapping into the wet area with the ⅜-inch (10mm) sable/synthetic angle. Move the paint toward the light (the top or right side of the stems) with a moist ½-inch (12mm) multitexture brush. Vary the bough color by adding touches of more opaque Burnt Umber, Burnt Sienna and/or the Maroon mixture. Let dry. Repeat for all stems. Let dry. Repeat to darken if needed.

6 Paint and Blend the Tops of the Leaves

Paint the leaves one at a time. Dampen the light area with the ½-inch (12mm) multitexture brush and clean water. Apply the Blue-Green mixture next to the flower and in the dark areas. With a clean, damp ½-inch (12mm) multitexture brush, extend the color over the light area. Quickly remove unwanted color with a cotton swab. Occasionally vary the leaf color by adding touches of watery Burnt Umber or Burnt Sienna. Repeat for all leaves except the bottom leaf, which should be applied very watery and undefined. In the same manner, dampen and then apply Burnt Sienna to the undersides of the curled leaves. Let dry. Dampen the leaves and stems, then add shadows cast by the overlapping petals. Use the Navy mixture and the background colors for the shadows. Direct shadows away from the flower with a clean, moist ½-inch (12mm) multitexture brush. Let dry. Repeat if needed.

7 Detail the Veins

Moisten the leaves, then paint veins on some of them using the no. 2 liner loaded with very watery Blue-Green mixture. Blot with your finger to subdue. Let dry. Remove the frisket from the outside petals.

8 Paint the Outside Curled Petals

Dampen all but the curled edge of a petal using the ½-inch (12mm) multitexture brush. Using the Maroon mixture loaded on the ⅜-inch (10mm) sable/synthetic angle, apply a very thin pale wash underneath the curled edge and along the side where one petal overlaps the other. Direct the flow of color toward the flower's center with a clean, moist ½-inch (12mm) multitexture brush. Using the Maroon mixture, apply a shadow where the petal connects to the calyx, directing the color flow toward the petal's center. Quickly remove the excess with a cotton swab. Repeat for all petals. Let dry. Remove the remaining frisket.

9 Shadow the Center Petals

Moisten the light areas of the center petals with clean water using the no. 2 liner. Using a watery Maroon mixture, apply watery maroon shadows, blending toward the light area. Let dry.

10 *Paint the Stamen*

Dampen the center of the stamen with clean water using the no. 2 liner, then apply Cadmium Yellow Medium to the edges. Allow the paint to travel toward the center. Remove the excess with a cotton swab. Create texture by adding tiny Burnt Sienna dibble-dabbles along the edge and near the calyx. Let dry.

11 *Add the Final Details*

Splatter the bottom with the background colors of your choice, using the no. 2 fan. Quickly remove excess color with a clean, moist sponge. Let dry. Sign your name. Try displaying your southern beauty in a 16" × 20" (44cm × 51cm) mat frame with glass to enjoy its beauty all year long.

Conclusion

I hope this book brings you many enjoyable painting experiences. I selected the subjects and techniques to give you a varied sample of the possibilities available to you. More are coming. *Painting With Brenda Harris, Volume 2: Precious Times* will be my next book. It will also offer you a wide range of subjects. Both books have accompanying PBS television series demonstrating how to paint the projects. If you are not receiving the shows on your local PBS affiliate, contact your station.

It has been a joy producing these books and television shows for you. I hope you will enjoy them all. I also hope to paint with you in person some day.

Sincerely,

Brenda Harris

Bearable
14" x 18" (36cm x 46cm)

Patterns

Grandpa's Little Angel
Enlarge this pattern 133 percent.

High Perch
Enlarge this pattern 153 percent.

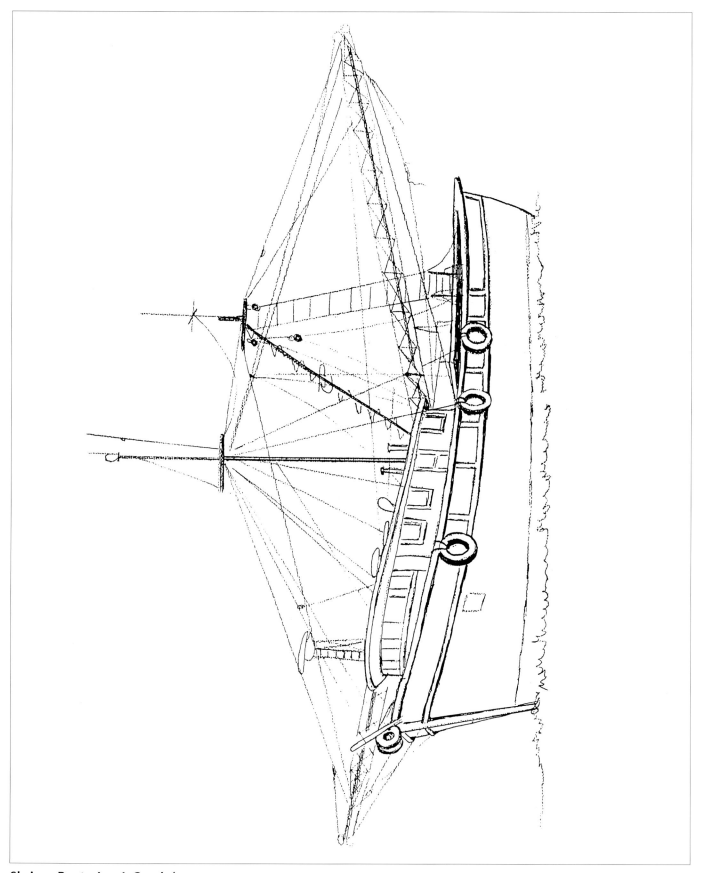

Shrimp Boats Are A-Comin'
Enlarge this pattern 155 percent.

Destin Dunes

Enlarge this pattern 154 percent.

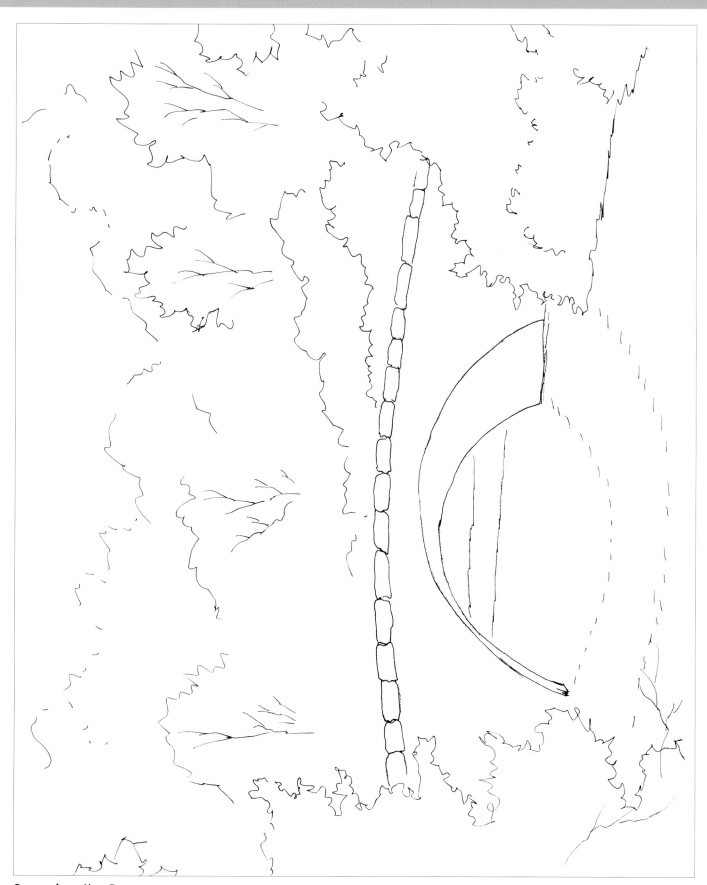

Someplace I've Been
Enlarge this pattern 153 percent.

Snow's on the Way
Enlarge this pattern 153 percent.

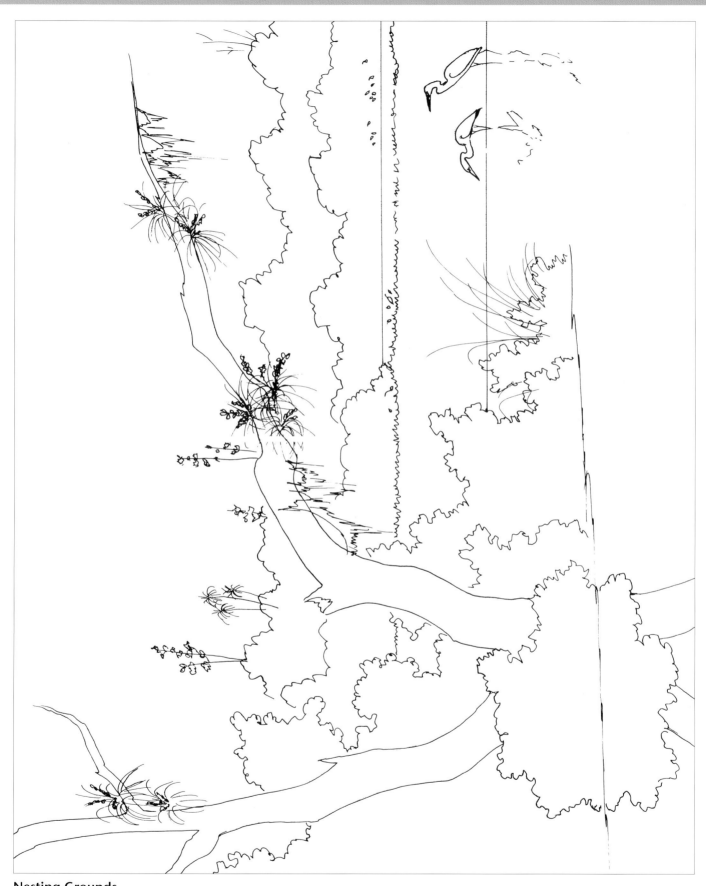

Nesting Grounds
Enlarge this pattern 166 percent.

A Special Place

Enlarge this pattern 188 percent.

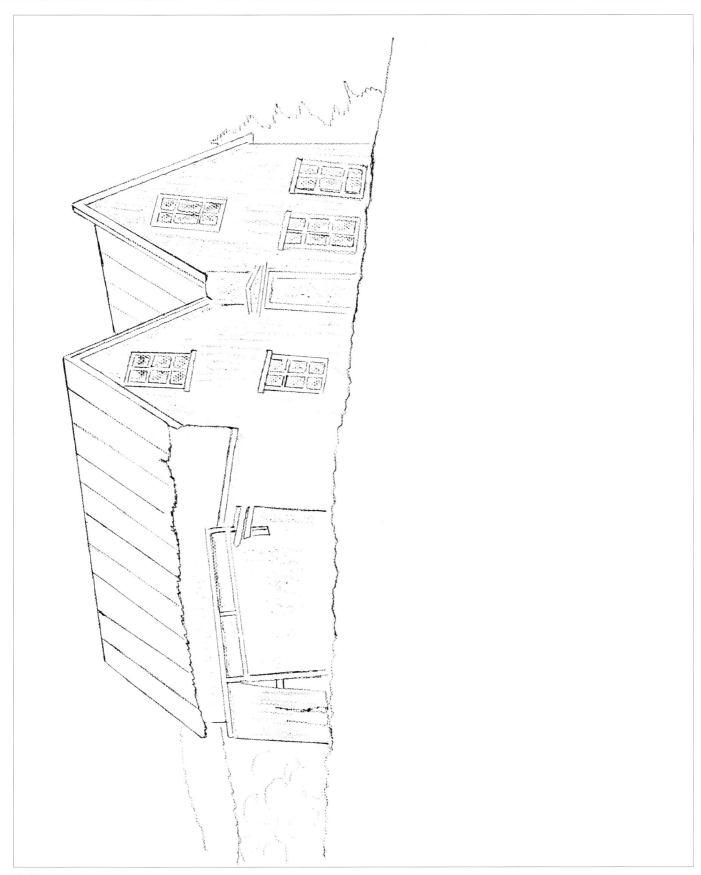

Twins

Enlarge this pattern 157 percent.

Bearable

Enlarge this pattern 183 percent.

Wonders of the Deep
Enlarge this pattern 200 percent.

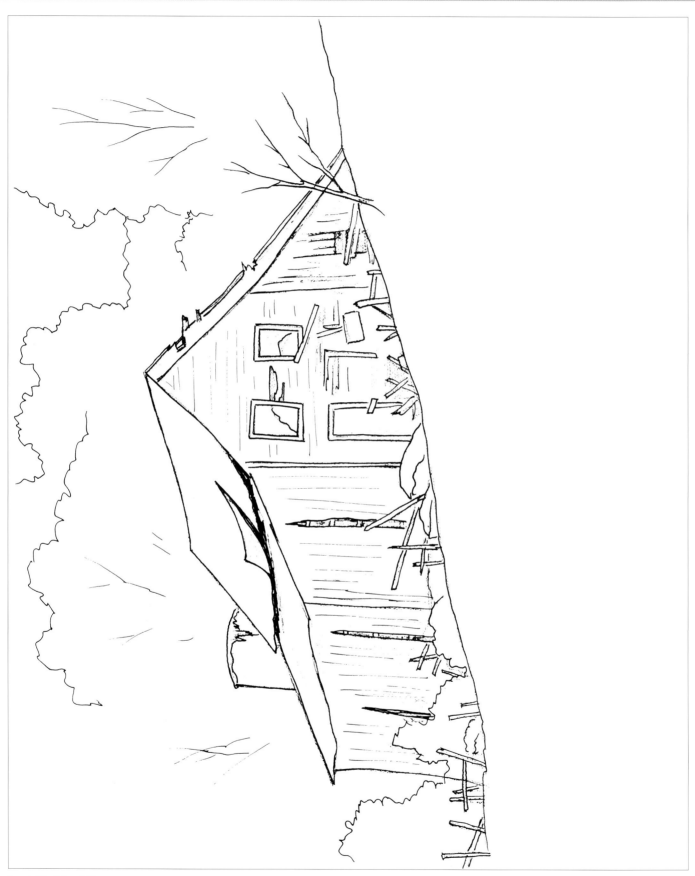

Last Light of Day
Enlarge this pattern 155 percent.

Southern Beauty
Enlarge this pattern 154 percent.

Index

Discover the best in fine art instruction and inspiration from North Light Books!

This book, the first in the Paint Along With Jerry Yarnell series, explores basic acrylic techniques. Jerry provides you with ten beautiful landscape projects, including a beautiful snow-covered road, a secluded forest path, a glorious desert, a quiet lakeside church and more.

ISBN 1-58180-036-3, Paperback, 128 pages, #31592-K

Travel with Jerry Yarnell through ten of America's most breathtaking landscapes—from mountain tops and rocky shores to farmlands and forests. Each project presents you with a fresh set of challenges to expand your landscape-painting repertoire and build your confidence. Instruction guides you through every step, from initial sketch to final adjustments.

ISBN 1-58180-180-7, Paperback, 128 pages, #31947

Learn how to properly execute basic acrylic painting techniques—stippling, blending, glazing, masking or wet-in-wet—and get great results every time. Jaqueline Penny provides five complete step-by-step demonstrations that show you how. Practice painting a flower-covered mountainside, sand dunes and sailboats, a forest of spruce trees and ferns, a tranquil island hideaway and a mist shrouded ocean.

ISBN 1-58180-042-8, Hardcover, 128 pages, #31896-K

Subjects from ponds to trees, and even the grass beneath your feet provide a world of animal images worth capturing with your brush. Stephen Koury shows you how to look beyond the ordinary to find them. You'll learn how to see beauty in even the most humble of creatures, then render them with incredibly realistic detail in a natural setting. Koury covers more than a dozen creatures in all, providing step-by-step instructions that enable you to recreate everything from translucent dragonfly wings to the damp, smoothly textured skin of frogs. It's all the instruction you need to paint nature's tiniest tenants!

ISBN 1-58180-162-9, Hardcover, 144 pages, #31911-K

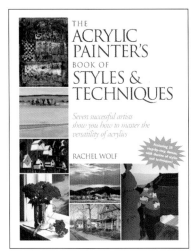

Enter the studios of seven acrylic artists! You'll find the inspiration to experiment with acrylics—and the techniques to help you succeed. This book brings together seven top acrylic artists, each of whom uses the paints differently to express their individual styles. You'll find 28 step-by-step demonstrations that showcase the methods that can help you master the many faces of acrylic painting.

ISBN: 1-58180-175-0, Paperback, 128 pages, #31935-K

These books and other fine art titles from North Light Books are available at your local arts & craft retailer, bookstore, online supplier or by calling 1-800-448-0915.